Visible Unity and Tradition

Max Thurian
Frère de Taizé

Visible Unity and Tradition

translated by W. J. Kerrigan

HELICON PRESS
Baltimore, Maryland

Helicon Press, Inc.
1120 N. Calvert Street, Baltimore 2, Maryland

Library of Congress Catalog Card Number 62–18771

Originally published in France by Editions de l'Epi,
under the title *L'unité visible des chrêtiens et la tradition*

**In the spirit of the World Council of Churches
and bearing in mind the Second Vatican Council**

PRINTED IN THE UNITED STATES OF AMERICA
BY GARAMOND PRESS, BALTIMORE, MARYLAND

Contents

Visible Unity of Christians

1 *Visible Unity of Christians*

INVISIBLE UNITY TODAY

God has revealed himself to us as unique and as triune—one single God in three persons. The problem of unity is presented—and solved—in God Himself. God realizes and lives in Himself the unity and singleness of divinity in three distinct persons. This is a trinitarian mystery too baffling for us to understand. But it at least allows us to realize (and this realization is of importance for our present subject) that uniqueness is essential to the divine nature and that, at the same time, this uniqueness is not solitariness, but a unity of three divine persons in one unique God.

God is the living actualization of the perfect unity of three persons—the Father, the Son, and the Holy Spirit. As unity and trinity he is the pattern of all unity in heaven and earth, and of the unity of the Church above all. For the three persons act in perfect harmony, in accordance with one common will and in full unity, yet are distinctly themselves with surpassing personal distinctness, the Father being only the Father, the Son only the Son, and the Holy Spirit only the Holy Spirit. In this way the members of the Body of Christ, the Church, must in all their multiplicity and all their individual distinctness one from another, tend towards that perfect harmony, that shared will, that full unity, which they contemplate in the Trinity.

God, this unity and trinity, knows all who belong to him in the invisible unity of the Body of Christ. For he, discerning the invisible thoughts and desires of men, can separate the weeds from the crop; he knows the ones to whom his Church extends, and sees the basic unity in which it embraces them.

In the act of creation, God willed the unity of creatures and of all humanity. His intention remains the same despite the sins of men and the disorder and division they have created among themselves and among creatures. God loves the universe he created in unity. And he sees it restored to unity through the sacrifice of Christ, for the effects of this sacrifice are universal and cosmic. Through Christ, creation and humankind have recovered the internal dynamism which unifies them under the eye of God.

The unity willed by God is as boundless as the universe. When we realize that this unity has been restored to the cosmos and to humanity in the sacrifice of Christ, and when we know that this hidden, invisible unity is nonetheless real, how tiny the visible divisions of the Church must seem. The internal tide which, since the cross, drives the whole universe and every human creature in it towards unity in and with God, cannot be stemmed or deflected by our petty ecclesiastical dissensions. The thought, then, of our paltry disputes being overwhelmed and swept under by the cosmic tide of unity in God must force us to view the external divisions of Christians in a more modest perspective.

It is for all men that Christ died; and the Spirit breathes where it will, gathering all men into the one single family of the Father. No ecclesiastical barriers of ours will prevent God from wishing all men in that family of his. That family, invisible to us and known to him alone, extends far beyond the lines drawn by our ecclesiologies and the pales erected by our excommunications. Thus the invisible unity of this wide family is one which no divisions we create can disunify. Blind to this unity, we often forget that it is there; yet there it is, a reproach to the scandalous differences which we should be composing.

Since the resurrection and ascension, Christ reigns as Lord over the whole world, and rules all things. Nothing escapes his rule, and he holds everything in the unity of his supreme government. The Church, since it can look upon itself only as the visible community of the Body of Christ, can recognize as Christians only those who profess its faith and participate in the sacraments of the faith. Yet, because of the mystery of God's will and God's providence, it understands that, outside its number, there are men who are oriented towards the Kingdom of God, and that these may one day be of that number. For it recognizes that all authentic truth and all real holiness, even in those who do not acknowledge Christ as Savior, must come from him, because there can be neither truth nor sanctity without him, and because he, as Lord of the world, has the governance of all men. Outside the limits of the visible Church, God is preparing hearts that will one day recognize him as wholly revealed in the Sacred Scriptures.

In view of these facts, the Church does not believe in its unity as an exclusive one, created through the elimination of everything which does not share the wholeness of Christianity. Christian unity is an inclusive one. It has its focus in the triune God—Creator, Redeemer, Inspirer—manifested in the whole of truth and holiness within the visible community of the Body of Christ; but it draws to itself and offers to God all things and all men outside this wholeness, for they belong to him.

Here there arises the problem of the non-Christian religions.

In every religion there is a tendency towards idolatry. Not even the Christian religion escapes this tendency; but it possesses the powerful means needed to exorcise it. Yet to say so much is not to say that all non-Christian religions are nothing but idolatry. First of all, some religions—whether possessing some of Revelation, like Judaism above all, but Islam as well, or touched by some light of the Gospel, like Hinduism—have really been explicitly affected by Christ's truth. Then still other religions, in their sincere desire for the right god, in their practice of prayer and in their rites of adoration, offer evidence that, even though not explicitly, the Creator and Lord of the world is mysteriously at work in them. The import of such random sparks of truth may escape us, but wherever they spring up it is our part to give glory to the fire of the Holy Spirit whence they spring.

In other words, the attitude of the Church towards all non-Christian religions, as towards itself, must be the desire (while attempting to banish every tendency toward idolatry and materialism) to bring to full flower in the unity of the Body of Christ whatever the Holy Spirit has begun (and here and there even developed). The Church cannot, glorying in its own sanctity, simply reject everything which happens to be outside its visible unity today; it must rejoice in truth and charity wherever found (for these can come only from Christ), and orient them towards the fulness of the Body of Christ. No confusionism, no indifferentism is implied in the foregoing assertion, nor suggestion that the fulness of truth and charity are accessible anywhere outside the visible Church, but only the fact that Christ, Lord both of the Church and of the world outside it, would lead every man towards the unity of his Body, by casting everywhere reflections of his light.

How—to give but one example—can we fail to recognize in Islam a reflection of the truth and holiness of Christ? True, Islam rejects the fundamental dogmas of the Trinity and the Incarnation; but in recognizing Christ as a teacher and prophet are not Moslems as close to the truth as certain Liberal Christians? Moslems and Christians have in common many elements of biblical revelation. Moreover, Islamic practice of prayer must edify us by the way it confronts the believer with God throughout every day. No, it is not confusionism to wonder whether Islam is farther from Christianity than some of the latter's sects or heresies. In the case of Islam as elsewhere, then, the Church must display its all-inclusive charity by discovering in Islam everything it has of authentic piety and holiness—truth which is capable of flowering in Christ. This is asking of the Church, instead of an attitude of conquest, simply one of attention and friendship. It is asking that the Church insure among Moslems the friendly presence of men and women who, in silence, prayer, and friendship, will share in as much of Moslem life as possible. In this way, little by little, whatever God intends from Christian and Islamic relations will be accomplished.

The Church cannot guess ahead of time what God intends for the world. It knows that Christ died for all men, and that he wishes them all in the unity of his Body. But how this redemption and this unity are to be applied to them the Church cannot foresee. All that is asked of it is to be itself: the Body of Christ, the presence here below of the humanity of Our Lord, God and man. It must extend the presence of this humanity of Christ everywhere, and, by means of its life in common and its profession of faith, offer itself to God as an obedient instrument for the work of the Holy Ghost among all men.

Towards those who, though calling themselves Christians, circumvent fundamental truths, or deny them, the Church must maintain this same open attitude. Of course, the Church cannot abstain from denouncing error; but it must always hope that wherever the Scriptures and baptism are to be found, there is always hope for unity—in fact, already a visible bond of unity. When two or three are gathered together in Jesus' name, he is there in the midst of them, according to his promise; and even if the Church cannot discern its own features in such a group, still it believes that the Lord is there just the same, at his work of unity. Whoever is not against Christ is with him, even when such a person dispels the unity and the efforts of the Church. So, though it condemn error in order to insure enlightened belief for its faithful, the Church must remain open to all who invoke the name of Jesus. It must believe that, by the Bible at least, they are all visibly united to it, and that this unity promises to become more and more explicit if, on its side, the Church succeed in renewing itself and advancing ever through conversion to Christ, the sanctification of the Spirit, and obedience to the Father of all.

VISIBLE UNITY TODAY

1) *Schisms in the visible Church have not destroyed all elements of visible unity.*

In the foregoing pages, we showed what unites Christians invisibly and fundamentally in the existence of the one God, Father, Son, and Holy Spirit, and in his design for all men, their assembly into the one family of the Father according to the original plan of creation.

In the pages which follow, we intend to show that there exists—and persists despite schisms—a *visible* Church unity on which we can base our efforts to seek and to find a still more extensive visible unity, which in turn will enable us to discern one single visible Church amid the rich variety of local and historical traditions.

To the divided Church at Corinth St. Paul asked the question, "Is Christ divided?" (1 Cor. 1:10–16). It is clear that in asking this question St. Paul was not thinking of the actual person of Christ in heaven (which would be absurd), but of Christ as manifested in his Body, the Church. For the apostle, the division of Christ's body is unthinkable and impossible, despite discords, divisions, and schisms. Just as it was Christ alone who was crucified for us, and not several saviors (Paul or anyone else), so the Church, the Body of Christ, is founded upon one fundamental and visible act alone: baptism in the name of Christ, baptism in the name of the Father and of the Son and of the Holy Spirit.

For St. Paul, unity of mind and purpose must be maintained, because there is but one Savior and one baptism: one Savior crucified and risen from the dead, who accomplished one redemption for all, whatever else separates them, provided they believe in him; one baptism in his name which visibly incorporates all Christians into the one visible Body of Christ. No division of Christians on other points—even very important points—can destroy this fundamental unity of the redeemed, and this visible unity of the baptized. In the face of dissensions, as at Corinth, Christians must return to their unity in Christ crucified and in baptism so as to discover anew the fulness of their unity, and all its potentialities. For that primitive unity will never be lacking among them, and it is in this sense that the gates of hell cannot prevail against the Church, which will always preserve the unity of its faith in the one Savior and of its baptism in him.

The question arises as to whether we can still speak of the Church of Christ where the Crucified is no longer thought the sole Savior nor baptism in his name habitually practiced. We take care to point out that no judgment on groups like, for example, the Quakers is to be inferred. They seem to us to enjoy—without themselves living the sacramental life—a kind of substitute grace due to their fraternal bond with the Churches. Theirs is, *mutatis mutandis,* a position analogous to that of the Eastern mystics who thought themselves able to dispense with liturgy and sacraments on account of their contemplative life. Their exceptional and often sanctifying existence is possible only in relation with the Churches which do practice the sacraments. The "spiritual" prophets of the Old Testament were possible only because a "traditional" cult had been established in Israel; they lived at second hand on its ceremonies, while at the same time spiritualizing it through their witness.

2) *Acceptance by all Christians of the Old and New Testaments is one of the chief forms of the Church's visible unity.*

St. Paul entreated the faithful of Corinth "in the name of Our Lord Jesus Christ" to remain in unity; for Christ is not divided; he is the *only Savior* of all, and it is in *his name alone* that all are baptized. Again, he wrote to the Ephesians: "There is but one Body and one Spirit . . . one hope . . . one sole Lord, one sole faith, one sole baptism, one sole God and Father . . ." (Eph. 4:4–6). There it is: one sole Father, one sole Son, one sole Spirit, living and revealing themselves in one sole church Body by virtue of its one sole faith and one sole baptism.

Despite schisms, then, the unity of one God in three persons, and the unity of one Body in many members are equally evinced in the unity of one faith and one baptism.

St. Paul was referring here, not to faith as catalogued in a series of analytical dogmatic theses, but to total faith—an englobing adherence of the whole being to God as he has revealed himself. This was the primitive faith in the name of the Lord. This true faith is given by the Holy Spirit, who enables us to confess the Son and possess the Father—to live in the Son and in the Father (1 John 2:20, 23–24; 3:23–24).

Our acquaintance with the name of the Lord, with his nature, his existence, and his will is given to us by his Word. This Word, announced under the Old Covenant and presented in the flesh under the New, has become embodied in the Scriptures. The Scriptures have caught in concepts and words, God's eternal Word to his people. In this sense, the Scriptures are a visible and audible body. The canon, or limit of the Scriptures in determinate chapters and books, was established in the interests of unity.

As a matter of fact, when the church community founded by Christ to safeguard and transmit faith in his redemptive name was first drawing its life from this living Word and handing it on orally and in writing, it did not at first fix a limit for its new Scriptures. Only the Old Testament was considered as complete and determined. The Gospels and the Epistles were still being written.

But when heresies sprang up, and with them certain writings false to history, the Church found itself constrained by the Holy

Spirit to reach a determination (canon) of the writings which were authorized and authentic. A New Testament was thus established along with the Old, and the Church limited its field of research into the Divine Word by putting aside the apocryphal fantasies of the heretics.

It was really in the interests of the unity of the faith and of the Church that the defined body of the Scriptures came into being. The Church, in reaching this important decision, was led by the Holy Spirit in the fulness of truth. The Church was confident that he it was who induced it thus to define the apostolic texts which from then on it was to recognize as the only inspired writings of the New Testament. This event was a sign that the Holy Spirit, far from leaving the Church to its own devices, took the initiative to preserve it in its essential unity, which consisted in professing God's name in the knowledge of the nature, existence, and will of its Lord. Both this profession and this knowledge it was thenceforth to be able to find in the Scriptures as a trustworthy witness of God's word, the history of salvation, and the wholeness of truth. Thenceforth it had only to contemplate its Lord in the faithful mirror of the Scriptures in order to reproduce, in its activities and in the charity which enlivened them, his image in itself.

Since all Christians everywhere acknowledge the inspiration (whatever the meaning they attach to the term) of the Scriptures, the fact that the Church's essential faith is to be found there (and that only there may they become acquainted with their only Savior) shows that the body of inspired writings is a visible institution of the Church. It is a form of Church unity not to be underestimated, since it is a gift of the Holy Spirit which preserves the Church's orientation in its beliefs.

To sum up so far: Scripture is a form of visible unity, persisting despite all schisms, and a sign that the Holy Spirit holds the Church together in its essential unity by visible forms such as this very body of inspired writings, and that he takes the initiative in preserving this visible unity when its foundations are menaced.

That the Holy Spirit gave the Church a body of inspired writings, a mirror wherein it might catch sight of the visage of its Lord, does not mean that he founded a religion on a book. If the unity of the Church had no more basis than that, it would be a static and lifeless thing. No, the Holy Spirit, having given the canon of the New Testament to the Church by making the Church the agency of its creation, continues to give life to the Word of God contained therein, to make it constantly pertinent and efficacious in the Church and in the world. Now Tradition is this unfailing life of the Scriptures in the Church through the invigoration of the Spirit. Tradition, indeed, is the life of the Church attentive to the Holy Spirit repeating ever afresh the Word of God.

Tradition cannot take the form of a canon of documents such as the Scriptures make up, for it is essentially the life of the Scriptures in the Church, whereas, if it itself were made static by being reduced to some rigid code, it in turn would require something to give it life; moreover, we should end up with two written sources of the truth. There is only one written and inspired source—the Scriptures. But there is a vital expansion of this source in every age in the Church, and this vital expansion is Tradition.

To understand the Scriptures as they exist in the Church, it is necessary to know the way in which the Holy Spirit has endowed them with life during the course of the centuries. We can have a scientific understanding of the Scriptures themselves according to the rules of exegesis and of history, but such an understanding is only partial; it tends to identify the Word of God with some specific age, and to canonize not only the Word, but also the age in which it was given utterance, so that logically the Church should simply go on copying the life it led in the beginning. The exegetical method is useful for a basic understanding of the texts in their original time and setting, but it can be completed only by a knowledge of an investigation of the way in which the Church has drawn from the Word of God contained in the Scriptures, throughout the various centuries.

Such an investigation can reveal to us the broader dimensions of God's Word, which is destined, not alone for one age (for in that case we should have simply to go on recopying), but for every age until the end of the world. This ampler notion enables us to reserve to exegesis its outstanding function of furnishing us with an understanding of the Word of God in the context of the historical period when—in the history of salvation—it appeared in the world. At the same time, not only to grasp the full significance of that Word as alive in every era of Church history, but also to keep an open mind to that same Word, in time to come, may under the action of the Holy Spirit disclose still more to us. The Holy Spirit does lead us to all truth, but to do so he takes what belongs to Christ (Scripture) and reveals it to us (Tradition).

Tradition, we may say, then, is a universal and ecumenical reading of the Scriptures by the Church in the light of the Holy Spirit. Only the Church's reading of the Scriptures can lead us into the fulness of God's Word. True, an individual theologian, exegete, or historian may bring particular light to bear on the interpretation of a given passage; yet such illuminations prove finally effectual only if they contribute to the understanding of the passage in question on the part of the whole Church, as guided by the Holy Spirit. Ultimately fruitful exegesis and theology must be associated with tradition and with contemporary ecumenical research, for a comprehensive insight into the Scriptures is conditioned not only by a historical, but also by a traditional and ecumenical reading.

Tradition, as the life of the Church, is perfectible. The interpretation of such-and-such a passage in Scripture may have been limited in the past by lack of knowledge of some fact of history, with the result that some modern historical or archeological discovery may lead the whole Church to a new understanding of that passage. Nor, of course, is our contemporary understanding of the Scriptures perfect, especially with our present state of division, and we must keep an open mind towards the ecumenical reading of the Scriptures, which is necessary to supplement our own limited knowledge. Let us repeat: the Word of God is for *all* the Church, and the Holy Spirit leads *all* the Church to *all* truth.

There is no question but that tradition has had its privileged moments—periods when the Church has been alert to the constant illumination of Scripture, or when Scripture was truly alive in the liturgy and in the Church's daily life. There can be no doubt that the first five centuries of the Church's history were such a period. It is for this reason that the first four ecumenical councils, and the study of the Fathers, occupy so important a place in our contemporary theological research. The ecumenical reading of the Scriptures in those first centuries may be said to have been realized as it has never been since; subsequent ecumenical reading, because of Church divisions, has been comparatively imperfect.

We are once again experiencing today, thanks to the biblical resurgence and the widespread ecumenical movement, unusual opportunities for an ecumenical reading of the Scriptures. The Tradition alive today in the Church, under the guidance of the Holy Spirit, is full of promise, for there exists among us all a desire for an ecumenical, non-polemical reading, one traditional instead of partial—a desire that betokens our common advance towards an ampler grasp of the whole truth.

We may therefore consider that we have here a visible form of our Christian unity: our common possession of a body of inspired writings towards which, more and more, all the Churches are orienting themselves as towards the fountain of living truth. Under the influence of the Holy Spirit we are coming to agree on a common text for our Scripture readings and in the ecumenical life of the whole Church.

3) *The visible incorporation of Christians into the Church through the sacrament of baptism is another of the chief forms of visible Church unity.*

The great majority of Christians mutually recognize the validity of one another's baptisms in the name of the Father, and of the Son, and of the Holy Spirit. This mutual recognition is another of the chief forms of visible Church unity. And among such forms it is all the more important since it is the sign and sacrament of the incorporation of Christians precisely into a visible Church—of their common membership in Christ's Body.

If we recognize the validity of the baptism of all Christians, then we must logically believe about their baptism, and about them as baptized, all that St. Paul asserts in the Epistle to the Romans (6:1–11).

We must recognize, that is, that by our common baptism all our Christian brothers have passed through the death, burial, and resurrection of Christ. They have all participated in Christ's great redemptive acts; they are one with him because they are dead and arisen with him. The one baptism we all have incorporates all Christians into Christ's very life—the "new life." Often when we turn our attention to our Christian brothers, to their Church, to their traditions, the thought strikes us that they are captives to a dead past, that they do not understand, as we do, the present-day pertinence of the Gospel, and that they are caught in the chill grip of dead institutions. But if we believe that that baptism has integrated them into the life of Christ, we must consider that in their Church and their traditions this new life of Christ is exactly what they are trying to lead. And then we may reflect that this new life, which is the life of Christ himself, cannot fail to produce through them in their Church the very work of resurrection which our thoughts had called into question. Through the baptized, dead and now risen with him, Christ himself, and the power of his resurrection, are even now at work in all the Churches.

Of course, the life acquired through baptism may be stifled by indifference and by infidelity. The Holy Spirit, champion of our faith, must be allowed to recall our baptism constantly to our minds. But this is true of all Christians—of us as well as of others. In the measure that the baptized live the life of their baptism—live in the faith which the Holy Spirit nourishes—they are power sources of the new life and possess the energy of Christ's resurrection with which to give life to their Church. They are in Christ; Christ, therefore, is with them, in their Church.

The baptized, because dead and arisen with Christ, bring both a death-dealing power over sin into their Churches, and a life-renewing power to the awakening of their Churches. Christ, who acts in them, acts through them to the end that sin may perish and life reawaken in their Churches. The baptism that Christians have in common, therefore, constitutes a splendid hope: Christ is truly present and active in all the Churches, to bring down to death the forces of division which lead to death, and to restore to life the forces of unity which lead to life.

But the baptism which Christians have in common is not only a hope that Christ is acting in each Church in the interests of unity; it is already, in its very existence as a universal visible sign, here and now one subsistent form of the visible unity of the Church, the Body of Christ. Since, by baptism, Christians pass through the death and resurrection of Christ, that is, become participants in the life and work of Christ and are united to him in a community of sacrifice and life, the unity with God which baptism creates unites them all together in God. By baptism, Christians are visibly one in Christ; they are visibly marked with the unity of the Body of Christ. Nothing can arise to endanger this fundamental unity; all that remains for them is to give it form in a common essential faith and in a common ministry.

That is why the unity of those baptized in Christ urges them on to ecumenical endeavors. Because they already possess that basic visible unity, it is absolutely necessary that they extend it ever more visibly. Thus efforts towards unity among Christians are not comparable to the organization of any merely human society, whatever it may be, or of non-Christian religions. Of course, human beings as such do form a real community, and further efforts ought to be devoted to exploring the implications and consequences of this human community in social life; but the community that Christians have in Christ by virtue of baptism is an entirely different thing. It boasts a sacramental visibility, pledge of an indestructible reality within: Christ himself uniting all the baptized in his Body and holding them together by the action of the Holy Spirit.

Would it not be well for the Churches to give greater emphasis, in the instructions they impart, to this visible unity of baptism, and to invite Christians, in their attitude towards their brothers of a different tradition, to express all the consequences of this unity in the fraternal interchange of a Christian community? For they are more closely united in Christ, visibly, by baptism, than they are separated in Churches divided by sin and by men's failure to grasp the fulness of truth and the unity it maintains amidst diversity.

This visible unity of baptism ought to give Christians full confidence that Christ, objectively present through baptism in all the faithful, hence in all the Churches, bestows new life upon each believer, and transmits it through him to each Church, thus uniting all the faithful together into the one Body of Christ, the visible Church. Unhappily, this visible Church, rendered one by the Scriptures and baptism, is divided into parties on the basis of diverse interpretations of the Scriptures; yet this unhappy situation does not—thanks to the visible unity of the Scriptures and of baptism—keep Christ from urging all Christians of good will to progress, little by little, towards a unity which will be more apparent to the world.

Of course, Christians there still are who through intransigence and through sectarianism refuse to take part in this ecumenical "movement" which is spreading more and more to all the

Churches, the Roman Church included. But if not in this refusal, where is "heresy" to be found today? True, each one of us still thinks that on such and such a point of faith such and such a Church is right, and another wrong. But, to the extent that we have the ecumenical spirit—the desire to achieve together one, same, more explicit, organic unity—we are moved to ask God's forgiveness for our divisions of today and to seek from him both the grace of beneficent discussion among separated faiths and the grace of unity in an ever-nearer tomorrow. No more for us the luxury of labeling others heretics in contrast with ourselves; for we must all of us go by the way of repentance and a change of heart if we are to arrive together at the state of unity which God desires.

If, in contrast, the sectarian spirit prevents us from entering resolutely into the ecumenical "movement," if we prefer to sit in judgment upon others and to remain sufficient unto ourselves, we fall into the sin of heresy in the very act of seeking to defend the truth and to turn other Christians into the way of salvation. For heresy today consists in denying the basic visible unity of all Christians through the Scriptures and baptism and in failing to take part in such ecumenical discussions as are alone able to obtain forgiveness for our persistent divisions. If, on the other hand, we accept the risks involved in these discussions, with both the sacrifices and the promises entailed, then we become brothers—separated still on many points, but fundamentally one in the Body of Christ, the visible Church of Christ which is founded upon a single body of inspired writings and constituted by the single corporate body of the baptized.

Our responsibility towards one another is a grave one. Instead of dissipating our energies in judging, criticizing, and debating—forms of the modern heresy—we should be sharing our Faith, aiding and defending one another against the common Enemy: the satanic forces of falsehood and division.

4) *Common prayers—the Our Father, the Psalms, the Apostles' Creed, the Nicene Creed—give expression to the visible unity of the Church today.*

In the prayer given us by Our Lord himself (familiarity leads us sometimes to say it without due consideration) we have a visible bond of our unity in the Body of Christ, a prayer which binds us together in one, common suppliant attitude towards God.

In the primitive Church, the Our Father was made the object of a solemn imparting (*traditio*) in the course of the Lenten instructions preceding baptism. The Church, after the previous long preparation of the catechumens, now placed upon their lips the Our Father, which they had a right to say with full-fledged Christians. The Church's permitting the baptismal candidates to say the Lord's Prayer with the baptized, and the solemn imparting thereof, emphasized the important churchly character of one, same, common prayer binding all Christians together in one same intention. The Roman rite today still prefaces the Pater Noster at Mass with an introduction traceable to that solemn primitive practice:

> Let us pray:
> Obeying our Savior's command,
> and taught by his divine institution,
> we dare to say: Our Father . . .

The Lord's Prayer, then, was conceived of as a divine institution *(divina institutione formati)* in which only those destined for baptism of water and of the Spirit could take part. The decisive churchly character of the prayer was thus emphasized. Only Christians incorporated into the Body of Christ by baptism can really say: "Our Father," for only the Church of Christ is really the family of God the Father, in the communion of the Holy Ghost. And those who thus dare to address God as their Father are bound to realize fully all that is implied thereby of the fraternal and family bond existing among them: none can now consider another an outsider, since all have become adoptive sons of the Father in Jesus Christ. Each must be recognized by all Christians as a son of their own Father, all of them brothers through the same relationship to the same Son of God, all the one same family, given life by the one same Spirit. All have the same intention and are petitioning for the same thing, in this common prayer.

Together, Christians call upon their common Father to provide for the hallowing of his name, that men over all the earth may recall that God is their sovereign Lord. By this common invocation Christians express their lively hope that the world will believe and glorify the Creator and the Savior. They commit themselves to the evangelization of the world, and orient the Church towards this evangelization. What good would it do them to be Christians if they forgot the salvation of other men? They cannot stand for the Gospel's belonging to themselves alone, but long to draw the whole world with them after Christ. In proportion to the universal conversion expressed in this petition, how petty their little divisions must seem to them! How much time lost in self-centeredness, with its attendant preoccupation with division and debate, while the whole wide world is waiting for the revelation of the children of God! The petition for the hallowing of God's name polarizes all the energies of the Body of Christ, directing them outward upon a world which stands waiting for the warmth of active Christian charity.

The petition to the Father for the coming of his Reign does as much to dwarf our divisions in comparison with the glorious expectation of the Kingdom. When Christians, in this petition, place the coming of the Reign of God in prospect, they are overcome by the grandeur of what they desire. They know that the coming of the Kingdom will mean for each one of them, first of all, the judgment. This judgment, based upon correspondence of life with faith, will not separate Christians according to their different creeds, but, unaffected by any such classification, will separate the weeds from the crop. For membership in a Church, even conceived of as the only Church of Christ, does not guarantee eternal salvation. We must live the Church's faith in charity if we are to possess the hope of everlasting life. Similarly, Christians whom we do not credit with the possession of a fulness of truth equal to our own will be judged on the correspondence of *their* lives with *their* beliefs.

The vision of the Kingdom, then, in this common petition of the Our Father, recalls to all of us the coming judgment and exhorts us to practice an authentic faith, a lively hope, and a real charity. On the last day we shall all be one before the judgment seat of God.

The vision of the Kingdom broadens our conception of the Church, however ample this conception may already have been. But the Kingdom infinitely surpasses the Church in glory, and the Church, in the presence of the splendor of the Reign of God at the end of time, will appear quite small, even though it is indeed the Body of Christ, the Spouse of Christ, the Column of Truth, the Temple of God, and the Presence of the Lord here on earth. And our divisions, in turn—how small they will appear when confronted with the immensity of the coming Kingdom.

The petition to the Father that his will be done on earth as it is in heaven is a real prayer for unity, and for a unity after his own mind. In this petition we find the essence of Christian prayer expressed. The one thing necessary, the one thing we ask in all our various prayers is that the will of God be done in all things. And we know that the unity of Christians is his will, for he expressed it through Christ in Christ's priestly prayer (John 17).

But to pray that the will of God be done is to proclaim his liberty. God's thoughts are above our thoughts; we cannot dictate our solutions to him; we submit to being led by him whither we should not have thought to go. Concerning his will for unity among Christians we know only that he cannot contradict himself, and, from revelation, that in faith and baptism he has provided an indefectible support for our unity; but the precise form of this organic unity is a secret of his will. We must possess our souls in patience, all with one mind giving ourselves up to prayer, until he lead us according to his will, enlarging our hearts and enlightening our minds.

How the will of God is done "in heaven" we do not know. But we know that his will is exerted fully, and that it is fully obeyed, in the perfect unity of the celestial hierarchy. That is why we ask that his will be done "on earth as it is in heaven." And as for the unity of Christians, which is a part of the will of God, we ask that it, too, be accomplished in accordance with his will—as he wills it and by the means he chooses—though the form of the accomplishment lie hidden beyond our limited horizons.

The proper attitude toward the unity among Christians willed by God is also reflected in the prayer for the kiss of peace in the Latin liturgy:

> Lord Jesus Christ, who hast said to thine apostles, Peace I leave unto you, my peace I give unto you; look not upon my sins, but upon the faith of thy Church, and in accordance with thy will bestow upon it unity and freedom from strife; who livest and reignest, world without end.

In this prayer, the "in accordance with thy will" refers both to Christ's expressed desire for the unity of the Church and to the divine choice of the form that unity is to take.

The petition to the Father to give us our daily bread unites all Christians in a solidarity thoroughly human. Christians they are, but they are also fully human beings, and it is well that they recall the fact in their prayers. Is it not a form of unity to be concerned about the nourishment and life of one's fellow man? Mutual aid among Christians may be a considerable factor in Church unity. If Christians ask their Father for daily bread for one another (and are willing to manifest the same spirit with concrete aid), this mutual concern may broach the psychological barriers between Churches, and open a corridor for spiritual commerce.

On the other hand, the cry for daily bread is not limited to Christians! But it is they who may—together—make a starved and underprivileged humanity their responsibility. Prayer and work for the well-being of all men is one work of human solidarity that all Christians together—as a unity—can and should undertake. In doing so, they will not be simply discovering a Christian activity they can work at in common without creating theological and ecclesiastical problems; they will also be engaged together in an act of unifying charity. Because they will be accomplishing together the will of their common Father, who furnishes the nourishment for every living being, they will find themselves already on the way to unity, a way which will eventually lead them to community both of belief and of the spiritual bread which they must share if they are to help still other fellow beings to live, not on bread alone, but on the Word which proceeds from the mouth of God. We say "must," for how can these fellow beings receive real nourishment from a Word that reaches them through the Babel of divided Churches? A hungry world awaits the daily bread and the Word of God uttered as it were in a single tongue by Christians united among themselves, if not yet totally, at least—in intention and good will—already visibly.

The petition to the Father for forgiveness has an unequivocal ecumenical bearing. Christians unite in asking that their sins against God be forgiven, that he forgive their debts. And what greater debt have they than the debt of unity? Christ gave us unity, and we have spent it, wasted it, lost it. We owe it to God, but we find ourselves unable to recover it in order to return it to him. Mere human efforts to recoup what has been squandered are in vain. We have left but one way out: to beg for mercy from our divine Employer, imploring him to forgive our misappropriations and malfeasances, and to keep us in his employment despite them. Only he, with his inexhaustible wealth, can restore to us what we have squandered. Restore it he will, but only if we are genuinely sorry for having lost it. He will give us back our unity only if we sincerely regret both our divisions and the causes past and present of our persistence in them.

We ask him to forgive our debts as we forgive our debtors. In this petition, we deliberately place a condition on the free forgiveness of God; that is, we oblige ourselves, as a condition of our being forgiven, to act as God does—to forgive the debts of those who are in debt to us. God has no need of this condition in order to forgive us, still, since in the petition we commit ourselves to forgiving as he forgives, woe to us if, being pardoned ourselves, we are harsh with our fellow men and exact from them what God does not exact from us. And therefore this prayer binds us divided Christians to forgive one another, in response to God's pardon pronounced upon our responsibility for our divisions.

We must forgive one another the trespasses we have committed as disunited Christians. The pages of history are black with such trespasses: polemics, recriminations, harassments, wars . . . even today we still hurt one another through lack of understanding, through theological disputes, through missionary rivalry, through unfair proselytism. We delight to see our separated brethren lose ground, and sometimes we even have the temerity to encourage them to break the promises they have made before God and their Church.

Not all the debts our brothers—and we ourselves—owe involve trespass, of course; they may be simply a failure, for example, to measure up to what is expected. Anyway, in all these matters, if our attitude is one of patience, of reluctance to pass judgment, and of readiness to forgive, we shall be acting in the ecumenical spirit and paving the way to unity.

The petition to the Father that we may not be led into temptation reminds Christians, united in this petition, to exercise vigilance against everything that may aggravate their divisions: chauvinism, politics, missionary zealotry. Now that we are on the way to unity, we must be on guard against such temptations and join together to ask that we might be spared them.

Finally, the invocation to the Father to deliver us from evil—an invocation pronounced by all Christians together—is like an exorcism of disunity.

The Our Father ends with a doxology proclaiming the kingdom, the power, and the glory of God, capable of lifting our hearts up into the intoxicating light of the Lord of glory, and thus of reducing to their just proportions our divisions and our oppositions; for these, however grave they may be, cannot tarnish the glory, slacken the power, or threaten the kingdom of the Lord. If we must not disguise from ourselves the difficulties that await us in ecumenical work, still our concern over them must be tempered through contemplation of the kingship, the power, and the glory of God, who has carried the victory, and shall still carry it, over the powers of evil and disunity.

Like the Our Father, the Psalms are a prayer which is part of the common property of all Christians and a visible form of their unity. The Psalms were Christ's prayer: they gave expression to his human spirituality; they were like a musical accompaniment to his ministry. Ever since, they have modeled the interior life of individual Christians and of Churches. How can they fail to help consolidate the Church's visible unity, giving, as they do, the same orientation to the prayer of all Christians?

Most Churches have made the Apostles' Creed and the Nicene Creed a part of their liturgy, their catechism, or their profession of faith. Of course, different Churches attach different degrees of authority to these texts. All the Churches at the time of the Reform, however, retained them as part of the patrimony of Christian faith, and preserved them in their liturgies and in their catechisms. The creeds, too, therefore, constitute a form of the Church's visible unity in faith. (That the Eastern Orthodox reject the insertion of *Filioque* in the Nicene Creed hardly affects the force of the present argument.) We may say, then, that the great majority of Christians, in the tradition of their Churches, profess the same fundamental truths and acknowledge identical summaries of the Revelation given in the Scriptures. We must thank God for having preserved our common essential faith in unchanged forms of expression in spite of schisms.

The authority of the ecumenical creeds is of course secondary to that of the Scriptures. It remains theoretically possible for a unified Church, some day, in a truly ecumenical council, to develop the Apostles' and Nicene Creeds, and, without contradicting them, to issue thus a third, new summary of the apostolic faith. With regard to Tradition the Church has a freedom which it cannot have in regard to the Scriptures. But this freedom in connection with the primitive tradition of the undivided Church expressed in the creeds is unthinkable save as associated with a truly ecumenical contemporary reading of the Scriptures—that is to say, in the framework of a council of the whole Church after it has regained its unity. It would be thoroughly temerarious for a particular, local Church to undertake to modify the creeds of the undivided Church. Would truth be found more readily in some present-day particular Church, separated from the other Churches, than in the primitive, undivided Church or than in the ecumenical, reunited Church of the future?

So long as lack of organic unity of all Christians prevents a literally ecumenical council, which is to say, until we are better informed, particular Churches may not touch the two Creeds. They stand as witnesses and as precious signs of unity of faith in the visible unity of the Church.

5) *The present-day ecumenical movement is responsible for certain provisional institutions which supply as signs of the visible unity of the Church until the day when they will yield their place to a universal conciliar structure which will express the total unity of Christians.*

The secretary general of the World Council of Churches, Dr. Visser 't Hooft, has on several occasions stated the fact that the ecumenical organization in Geneva in no way constitutes a superchurch having power of authority over the various Churches connected with it. The World Council provides a place and opportunity for Church members to meet freely for friendly discussion and common inquiry on the subject of local unity for Churches in the same locality, and universal unity for various ecclesiastical traditions in an ecumenical structure which will stand as a sign of the total unity of Christians.

The theological work of the World Council consists, after a period of comparative theology, in engaging theologians of different faiths in joint research on the evident doctrinal content of the inspired writings which unite all Christians—the Scriptures. They undertake together an ecumenical reading of the Scriptures, convinced that more light is cast when Christians lend themselves to joint investigation than when they allocate themselves in separate traditions, ignoring one another. This ecumenical reading of the Scriptures consists in profiting from all the past and present experience of the Church in its understanding of the Word of God. This does not involve anyone's renouncing his own tradition (but only of divisive particularisms); rather, it is an effort to bring the tradition of each to flower in ecumenical unity.

In the present state of division among the Churches, the World Council, though not endowed with authority over them, provides for a provisional ecumenical bond among them, a contact which would normally be established by a conciliar meeting of the bishops (or equivalent functionaries) of the various local Churches throughout the world. (In Churches with an episcopate, this ecumenical activity is exercised by bishops, each of whom, besides giving unity to and ruling his local Church, keeps it in communion with other Churches throughout the world and thus renders ecumenical unity vital. Churches without an episcopate should still provide for this activity, lest local Churches become particularized, nationalized, and cut off from communion with other Churches, thus preparing the way for further divisions. This activity—which we may style "ecumenical ministry" or "ministry of catholicity"—was exercised in the Church from the outset by the apostles. St. Paul's journeyings and epistles, the pastoral epistles—these witness to the necessity of the exercise of this vital ministry for the ecumenical unity of local Churches and for the tonic effect upon these Churches provided by ecumenical contacts.

In their divided state before the appearance of the ecumenical movement, the separated Churches no longer possessed a ministry of catholicity with the function of maintaining communion between the local Church and other Churches; or if they did possess it—

as did Churches with an episcopate, for example—it was frustrated by schisms and controversies.

The World Council, without pretending to be an ordinary institution of the universal Church, has enabled this ecumenical ministry of local Churches to be reborn or to regain its function. Every Church that is a member of the World Council, through representation at general meetings, on theological commissions, and sometimes on the permanent board at Geneva, has witnessed the revival of its ecumenical function or ministry of catholicity. Local Churches, if they possess no organ of this ministry in the episcopate, delegate pastors or theologians, or create ecumenical commissions, and thus establish, through the World Council, a circulation of life, thought, and information between themselves and other Churches.

The World Council has thus revived the exercise of the ecumenical ministry in and among the Churches—a ministry essential to their universal communion and their local refreshment. In reviving this traditional, apostolic, New Testament activity, the World Council, without being an ordinary institution of the Church, has caused the reappearance of a sign of the Church's visible unity: the ministry of catholicity, episcopal or non-episcopal.

Thus one may say, without exaggerating the ecclesiastical standing of the World Council, that it constitutes, as a provisional institution, a sign of the Church's visible unity in that it gathers together the ecumenical organs of the local Churches and provides them with contact in life, thought, and prayer. Of course, this contact falls short of the plenitude of the general council which will be possible when the Church has recovered its total unity; nevertheless it is already a manifestation of progress towards organic unity. One might say that the World Council of Churches is the adumbration of the World Council of the *one* Church, and thus, like any other shadow, already an indication, and, however provisional and precarious, a sign of the visible unity of the Church.

The World Council, in enabling Churches to exercise the ministry of catholicity, also enables them to profess together a common faith. In this connection we note that the doctrinal constitution of the Council, at first purely christological, is undergoing, upon the request of some Churches, some modification in a more trinitarian direction. The following text is due to be submitted to the Churches for approval:

> The World Council of Churches is a fellowship of Churches which confess the Lord Jesus Christ as God and Saviour according to the Scriptures and therefore seek to fulfill together their common calling to the glory of the one God, Father, Son and Holy Spirit.

The existence of a doctrinal constitution, of a common profession of faith for the Churches which make up the Council, is likewise a sign of visible unity. Of course, the sum total of faith is not expressed therein, nor even the maximum amount possible, nor indeed all that is necessary for unity of the Churches. But we do find there the profession of essential faith: God, Father, Son, and Holy Spirit; Jesus Christ, God and man, Lord and Savior, according to scriptural revelation. In fact, do we not find expressed succinctly there what the first four Ecumenical Councils of the undivided Church expressed at greater length as the revelation of the Scriptures on God and the incarnation?

The first four councils were proclaiming the common faith of the Church, as a sign of its unity. The World Council of Churches in epitomizing this common faith has produced a new sign of visible Church unity.

Thus we may say that the World Council of Churches offers a sign of visible unity that has both a "conciliar" character (revival of the "ecumenical ministry" or "ministry of catholicity" in the Churches) and a "doctrinal" character (epitome of the scripturally-based common faith of the yet undivided Church).

Other alliances and federations of Churches are also signs of visible unity. Possibly they represent some form of the limited, local council, adapted to the present-day condition of divided Churches. Church history chronicles a number of local councils, summoned to settle problems which concerned a group of local Churches.

Of such groups today, the alliances embrace Churches claiming the same spiritual tradition, distinct from other traditions in the universal Church: the Anglican Communion, the Presbyterian Alliance, and the Lutheran Federation, for example. Geographical limits are here replaced by limits of a particular tradition. However, to the extent that these alliances serve, not the restricted unity of an individual tradition, but a more catholic unity of the whole Church—as did the local councils of history—they may be useful means to the end of a conciliar recombination in the universal Church. They should guard against impeding or preventing mergers of various Churches in any locality, for the unity of the Church in any given place, to the extent that it remains open to the ecumenical unity of the whole Church, is more important than bonds of a particular tradition such as are found in the various alliances. To the extent, then, that the alliances favor both universal unity and local unity, they may be considered interim forms of the local council, adapted to present-day divisions, which follow lines both of geography and of belief.

As distinct from the alliances, the national federations have still more the character of a local council, for they embrace various Churches of the same country in order to co-ordinate their efforts in various fields of common interest. If their collaboration is limited to purely practical problems, their role is not that of a local council; but if, by means of a serious theological collaboration, they tend to banish what divides them into separate faiths, and resolutely aim at local, and national, and complete unity while preserving the rich variety of desirable differences, then they are a real form of the local council, adapted to conditions of present-day divisions. But here again, what must take first place is unity—the ecumenical unity of the whole Church, and local unity. Like the world alliances of particular traditions, these national federations of different Churches must look forward to withering away as there appears and develops the superseding unity of a group of Churches in a real local council, along with the unity of all the Churches in a real ecumenical council.

VISIBLE UNITY TO BE RECOVERED

Vestiges of visible Church unity—or elements of that unity already restored, even though in precarious or interim forms—are not to be underestimated; but it is easy to see that we still have a long way to go if we are to recover those lost elements of unity which, though preserved here or there, have not been retained all together by all Christians. Our next task here, then, is to pick out these necessary elements, without which, despite its basic unity, and visible though this be in certain important regards, the Church cannot be recognized as the one, single community which embraces all Christians in one same faith and communion.

1) *Conciliar faith.*

Like both the Roman Church and the Orthodox Church, the Reform Churches, in the sixteenth century, accepted the authority of the first ecumenical councils. They admitted that the trinitarian and christological proclamations of the first four councils—Nicaea, Constantinople, Ephesus, and Chalcedon—accurately interpreted the Sacred Scriptures. The various Reform professions of faith reasserted these dogmatic definitions without qualification. And the Reform theologians of the seventeenth century even made it a point of honor to show themselves stricter adherents to this faith of the early Church of the first five centuries than Roman Catholic theologians were.

It was in the subsequent centuries, of the Enlightenment and then of Romanticism and religious liberalism, that these first conciliar dogmatic proclamations were called into question, being criticized as Hellenistic, out of accord with the pure Gospel, and vainly attempting to submit the faith of the heart to intellectual formulas. The two great creeds themselves disappeared from liturgies and from catechisms. In allowing this, Reform theologians (or Reform Churches) departed from their own authentic tradition and ceased to accept what the Reformers, and seventeenth-century theologians, had recognized as being beyond discussion. For by their acceptance of the first four ecumenical councils as faithful interpreters of the Scriptures, the Reformers and their immediate successors had implicitly acknowledged the high value of the ecumenical interpretation of the Scriptures in the early Church.

This "world-wide reading" of the data of revelation, or of the Sacred Scriptures, which an ecumenical council supplies, is a vital factor in the unity of the Church. The "ecumenical interpretation" supplied offers the greatest possible certitude, in the concrete situation, of laying hold of the Truth contained in the

Scriptures. One council can always go further into, or make more explicit, something defined by a preceding council; but it is not thinkable, save the exception of a case of prophecy (which only God can identify surely), that an individual should be right as against a truly ecumenical council. Thus, so long as the universal Church is not assembled in a really ecumenical council to make more explicit, go more deeply into, or enlarge upon the proclamations of those earliest councils, it is hard to see how some particular Church, much less some private theologian, could possibly call into question those fundamental trinitarian and christological dogmas promulgated with all the authority of the one and universal Church.

(At this point one may wonder why Reformation professions of faith generally embraced nothing after the first five centuries and the Council of Chalcedon, whereas, for example, the Orthodox Church recognizes the authority of the first seven fully ecumenical councils. Perhaps the Reform Churches did act inconsistently here; or perhaps they felt that it was the first four councils that were of major importance, since they had given complete fundamental form and security to trinitarian and christological biblical faith. In any case, to go further into this particular point would exceed the scope of the present study. What matters to us here is that the historically existent Churches, up to the sixteenth and seventeenth centuries, conceded the authority of the first four ecumenical councils as authentic interpreters of the Scriptures.)

Of course, some Churches emphasized this conciliar authority more than did others, ranking it with the Scriptures, or subordinating it to the Scriptures; but the important point is that they did recognize it. Therefore, to call into question these four councils and their definitions is to depart from a long and uninterrupted tradition of the Church. Only another truly ecumenical council could have the authority to develop these definitions interpretively.

Since a really ecumenical council will consist of a meeting of all the Churches, until this can be accomplished Christians must strive to recover the common conciliar faith of the early Church. This is a second and necessary step towards visible unity of faith, which, as we have noted, has already been achieved on some fundamental points. To some minds this talk of recovery of an earlier faith will bring dismaying thoughts of a crotchety antiquarianism. No, the question is not of acquiring a passion for antiques, but simply of setting out, in accordance with common sense, at a point where the trail has already been broken for part of the way.

In this effort we may also be called upon for intellectual sacrifices. Well, our individual and collective sacrifices are the price of Church unity, after all. This effort to recover allegiance to conciliar faith does not, of course, exclude liberty of theological, historical, and critical research. But, instead of considering the whole history of the Church as placed at the disposition of our theological investigation, to be judged freely, in the light of our modern criteria, we shall allow a sound ecclesiology to force us to acknowledge that at certain privileged moments, constituted by the general councils, it seemed good to the Holy Spirit and to the Church to interpret the Scriptures in the form of dogmas universally recognized as corresponding accurately to revealed data, because the whole Church was present to seek the truth in unity. This primacy of the "ecumenical reading" of the Scriptures over interpretation by a particular faith or a particular individual is a necessary principle for all real ecumenical work. And since Church tradition sets us the example and offers us the successful results of this "ecumenical reading," one of the first steps in pursuit of the visible unity remaining to be recovered is for us humbly to adopt as goals already achieved the dogmas of the first four councils.

If, in contrast, these dogmas are constantly to be placed in question, how can we ever reach an understanding in a new ecumenical council after the divisions, since we cannot come to an understanding on the authority of the first councils, before the divisions? This act of faith is asked of us until further inquiry, that is, a new ecumenical council, making perhaps more explicit some dogmas already defined. But until that time we have no better access to the truth contained in Sacred Scriptures and believed in by the whole Church than the trinitarian and Christological dogmas of the first councils. Rather than a critical attitude towards what to some seems to have been a school of thought which hellenized the revealed data, what is required of us is grateful submission to the Holy Spirit, who has guided the Church into truth, and will continue to guide it, if it seeks unity and unanimity.

The rediscovery of this unity of conciliar faith on the part of all the Churches is also demanded by the urgent nature of the Church's mission in the world and by the requirements of its pastoral office. In view of the Church's universal mission, and of the urgency of this mission, it is of paramount importance that Christians regain the fundamental faith that they once proclaimed unanimously and that all the historical traditions up until the seventeenth century formally sanctioned. For how are Christians to hope that their testimony will produce any results in the world if they refuse even to recover an expression of faith which formerly enjoyed centuries-long unanimity among them? They are wasting their time in bringing back into question this or that expression in the common creeds while all the while the world is waiting for a clear and simple word which will deliver it from its darkness and bring it new hope. The seriousness of the Church's business in the world should constitute an imperative prohibition against any Christian's bringing into question the common conciliar faith of the first five centuries. Christians cannot go on forever in narcissistic indolence while the suffering millions of their fellow men hunger for material and spiritual bread. There is an orthodoxy which the specifications and the urgency of the Church's mission render, not static, but living: to transmit the Word of life more freely, the Church needs clear and simple dogmas; to transmit it efficaciously, it needs unity—the unity of conciliar faith.

In its pastoral function among its own, the Church also needs to recover the living faith of the first ecumenical councils. The Church cannot permit the faithful to be blown hither and thither by every wind of doctrine; it has a doctrinal responsibility, which consists in teaching the faithful to preserve everything which Christ taught. And this deposit of teachings which they must cling to, the deposit of faith contained in the Sacred Scriptures, has been epitomized in the two great creeds and presented in detail by the ecumenical councils. The Church, anxious both to preserve the apostolic faith in the hearts of its members and to build them and all their Christian brethren throughout the world into a unified structure, will submit quite naturally to the rule of faith laid down by the first ecumenical councils. In so doing, it will accomplish efficacious catechetical work and durable ecumenical work. It will, that is, fulfil simultaneously its pastoral ministry and its ecumenical ministry.

The Church would be building on sand, and would be lacking

in genuine pastoral concern, if it abandoned the faithful to the freedom of their own religious ideas, their own interpretations of the Scriptures, their own individual fancies, or if it failed to protect them against the dangers of theological research more anxious for "scientific novelties" than for coherence with the Church's viewpoint, is "pseudo-scientific." In fact, Christian truth study is necessary to give constant refreshment to the Church's faith, if theologians must enjoy a certain scientific liberty, they cannot still hope to discover religious truth without the Holy Spirit. And where the Holy Spirit works is in the heart of the Church, at building up the faithful unto unity and charity. There exists a purely "scientific" conception of theology which, from the Church's viewpoint, is "pseudo-scientific." In fact, Christian truth is not to be found at the bottom of an historical and exegetical investigation, however searching and however honest it be. Such investigation—necessary, of course, if we are to know the human milieu, the historical circumstances, and the prevalent literary genres which brought Revelation into the world—must, if theological effort is to be really scientific, in accordance with God's own knowledge, be grafted ever anew into the communion of the Church.

Scientific truth in theology is a conclusion from scientific exegesis controlled by the rule of faith laid down by the Church in the ecumenical councils, for the most accurate interpretation of the Scriptures is that of the whole Church, in ecumenical communion with the first readers of the Scriptures—the Fathers. That is the dependable scientific truth towards which the Church's theological effort is directed. Without this ecumenical continuity insured by the Holy Spirit present in the Church met in council, theology, even in the sense of serious scientific exegesis of biblical texts, cannot be certain of having attained scientific truth. The matter may be epitomized thus: *theological science is composed of exegesis and of submission to the faith of the councils.*

In matters of faith, then, the Church does exercise a magisterium, which is not some facile guarantee of a precarious intellectual unity, but the very expression of its pastoral office, designed to protect the valid deposit of faith, so that the weakest of God's people may be strengthened by the truth that is in Christ Jesus, and be built up unto ecumenical unity by the Holy Spirit.

A reconsideration of the first four ecumenical councils is due, then, among Churches seeking to develop their visible unity. In the conciliar trinitarian and christological dogmas they can find an expression of their common biblical faith. And this conciliar rule of faith can enable their theological effort to orient itself more securely towards plenary truth. Like the early Fathers of the ecumenical councils, present-day Churches can beseech the Holy Spirit to establish continuity between them and the thought and determinations of those first councils, so that when the day arrives for a truly ecumenical council they will possess—in common interpretation of Scripture, in fundamental dogmas, and in the essential truths concerning the Trinity and Christ—a solid and trustworthy starting point.

The part played by the biblical revival in all the ecumenical work of the past several years must not be underestimated. There is no denying that after the Lund Conference ecumenical theological work made marked progress because the representatives of various faiths there agreed to turn again—with minds as free as possible—to the Scriptures as to a mine of truth.

However, as things stand now, we shall run into difficulties without solution if we do not discover a new discipline for scriptural reading. In fact, when Christians of separated faiths approach the Bible together, for each of them there inevitably arise questions of interpretation—the problem of hermeneutics. Three groups holding contrary viewpoints are bound to appear:

One group will assume that the Bible—specifically, the New Testament—must be understood from the point of view of a central message, of a *kerygma.* For these, the New Testament is not binding upon us except to the extent that it reveals the Lord to us—to the extent that it is to be understood in the light of what is necessary for our salvation. These Christians tend to make a distinction between permanent, normative essentials and temporary accidentals. For example, everything concerning the incarnation and redemption, justification by faith, and sanctification will be of capital importance for them; but data on the hierarchy of the Church, on the ministry, will seem to them temporary, and not normative for the present-day Church.

A second group of Christians will understand the New Testament from the point of view of the apostolate, conceived of as the extension in time of Christ's humanity and of his authority. For these Christians, not only Christ's words, and whatever concerns his person, his work, and our salvation, but also the activities of the apostles are normative today. For them, the organization of the Church, as revealed in certain passages in the Acts of the Apostles and in the Epistles, is part of what is to be considered normative in the New Testament. Of course, these Christians do make a distinction between elements peculiar—in the plan of salvation—to a particular time, and permanent elements, which retain their validity in the Church throughout the centuries; thus they connect certain miraculous phenomena to the period of revelation, during the lifetime of the apostles, and do not consider these extraordinary activities as having to be reproduced in the Church today.

Still a third group will take the whole Bible—or at any rate the New Testament—on a single level, judging that not only what concerns Christ and salvation, and what the apostles indicated about the organization of the Church, but also all the extraordinary, miraculous phenomena contained in the New Testament are normative and necessary for the Church in every age.

Thus, even when we come to the Scriptures, we are divided in our ways of interpreting them. If, therefore, we are to make progress towards unity, we must bring into practice the universal reading of which we have already spoken, and seek out, in the first centuries of the Church, some guideposts to aid us in this understanding. As a matter of fact, the trinitarian and Christological dogmas of the first four ecumenical councils are well suited to guiding our understanding of the Scriptures, and to providing a control of our biblical theology. After the meeting on Faith and Order at Lund, there was general agreement among members of the theological commissions to approach the Scriptures together, using the trinitarian and Christological interpretation provided by the first centuries of the Church. This was a recognition of the fact that our reading of the Scriptures must be guided by a theological system faithful, of course, to the Scriptures themselves, but elaborated in the course of the first centuries of the Church and defined in the ecumenical councils.

But why should we accept only theological—trinitarian and Christological—guidance from this source? Why should not the structure of the Church as it was known to the first centuries guide us just as usefully to an understanding of the Church as it was revealed for us in the New Testament? Why should we not consider the episcopal ministry, as it developed in the early Church, an authentic interpretation of the pastoral epistles? And, finally, if we accept the Christological and ecclesiological interpretations, shall we not consistently recognize in the liturgical practice of the early Church highly useful, and even necessary, guideposts for the present-day Church's attainment of the truth contained in the Sacred Scriptures? Has the way in which a Hippolytus, or later an Ambrose, understood the liturgical mystery nothing to teach us about an adequate conception of the sacraments and the ministers of the Church?

The fact is that the Church Fathers of the early centuries were the first readers, the first interpreters, of the gospels and the epistles. Are the Fathers, then, not indispensable to us if we are to discover the ecumenical reading of the Scriptures, and to understand what the Scriptures have to teach us not only about trinitarian and Christological dogmas, but also about ecclesiology and the liturgy? Today we have come to see that it is impossible to make a radical distinction between the first century and the centuries which followed; for there is no discontinuity, for example, between the century of the apostles and the second century of the Church. Men simply followed one another. Take Irenaeus of Lyons, for example. He was in direct touch with Polycarp of Smyrna, who, in turn, had known St. John. About forty years after the organization of the Church in the region of Ephesus by St. Paul and Timothy, St. John exercised his apostolic authority there, at the same time as St. Ignatius was commencing his episcopal ministry at Antioch. And all this apparently without the least discontinuity.

For this reason we may say that that structure of the Church as we find it in the second half of the second century can no longer be held to be in formal contradiction with the structure of this same Church as set forth in the New Testament. It is highly necessary to be aware of this concrete continuity in the early Church, in order to avoid assuming some break between the age of the New Testament and the age of the Church. The picture of a golden age of the Church followed by successive ages of infidelity is a false one. Of course, the revelation contained in the New Testament occupies a place of its own, but it cannot be understood unless it is grasped as implicated, in this continuity, with the early Church which preached it—and was the first to do so.

To achieve the ecumenical reading of the New Testament of which we have been speaking in this volume, we must take into account the first centuries of the Church and grasp what they have to show us as regards their dogmatic teaching on Christ and the Trinity, their ecclesiological teaching on the structure, organization, and different ministers of the Church, and, finally, their liturgical teaching, which shows us how the Church prayed in conformity with the Scriptures. The early centuries of the Church, and the first four councils at least, are bound to reveal to us their legitimate continuity with the New Testament. If we do all this, we are simply doing what all Christians did, at least until the seventeenth century.

As already explained, the attitude just described has nothing to do with any kind of antiquarianism; it is no passion for antiques or antiquities that leads us to return to the early Church to try to understand how it read the New Testament, how it preached, how it lived. If we return to the early Church, it is because there is an imperative call today for Church unity; it is, furthermore, because the world demands that we heed the urgency of that call; and how are we going to achieve this unity if we do not return to its source, which is in Christ, revealed by the New Testament and lived by the Church of the first centuries in conformity with the New Testament?

2) *Unity of the ministry.*

The problem of the ministry is one of the most delicate in the quest for visible unity. In fact, for Churches of the "Catholic" type, the validity of the sacraments depends upon the manner in which the ministry has been ordained, and upon the minister of the ordination. It is therefore evident that the accomplishment of visible unity in sacramental intercommunion involves sooner or later the problem of the ministry.

Note that this is not the same as the problem of Church government. The form of Church government does depend on ecclesiological and theological factors, but the way in which this government takes form in a given time and place is highly dependent upon non-theological factors. This is to say that any government the Church may have does have to have a form which manifests the fact that it is Christ, as Head, who governs his Body from above, and that it is the Holy Spirit who gives life to the structure of the Church and is the bestower of the various ministries.

But there are certainly many ways of manifesting this government by Christ and the Holy Spirit from above; and these ways vary from time to time and from place to place, depending on non-theological factors. This is a matter in which the Church must not be narrow, but permit diversity. What is essential is that in any of these forms of government Christ be really recognized as the Head, governing from above, and the Holy Spirit as the Life-giver, whose activity extends throughout the body, permeating the whole of God's People. If we may be forgiven an ugly neologism, we may say that the Church's system of government, whatever the accidental forms it takes, is a "demotopneumatic christocracy": the power resides in Christ, who exercises it from above, through the ministers; but this power also necessarily resides in God's People taken as a whole, the life-principle of whom is the Spirit who lives and expresses himself therein.

The problem here, then, is not so much Church government as Church ministry, as a visible sign of Christ's activity and as a visible sign of unity.

Nor are we dealing here with who is right: the "Catholic" Churches, which recognize a separate priesthood, or the "Evangelical" Churches, which recognize a universal priesthood. This contrast, besides being oversimplified, is full of surprises: we find some "Catholic" Church assigning an important place to the laity, and at the same time some "Evangelical" Church at a loss how to use the faithful and concentrating all ministerial functions in the pastor.

But it is worth noting that the theology of the ministry has evolved considerably in the various traditions. Thus, in the "Catholic" Churches the notion of a "separate priesthood" is being modified in favor of the conception of a "ministry of the priesthood of Christ," simultaneously with the development of a theology of the Mass as a "sacrament of sacrifice," and no longer as a "separate sacrifice." Everything is much more clearly focused on Christ as the one priest and one sacrifice, "sacramentally" present and living in the priesthood of the Church, in the preaching of the Word of God, and in the eucharistic sacrifice.

At the same time, in the "Evangelical" Churches the return to the sources of the Reform has resulted in a more profound notion of the ministry, namely, the biblical conception of a royal priesthood of the whole Church organized in various ministries.

Despite real differences among the Churches in those regards, the decisive and persistent divergences are to be found not so much among views of the ministry in relationship to the laity (it cannot be said that there are clerical Churches and lay Churches; this is a false opposition); the decisive and persistent divergence lies rather in the acceptance or rejection of the episcopal ministry, understood not only as a headship, but as the ministry of unity.

What constitutes essentially the character of the episcopal ministry is ordination for the unity of the local Church in itself and for unity of the local Church with the universal Church. The Church has changed and may still change as regards privileges reserved to the bishop, like that of being the ordinary minister of certain ecclesiastical functions: today, the Roman Church itself permits confirmation to be administered in certain cases by priests. If, in "Catholic" Churches, the ministers are "validly" ordained by bishops, this is not by virtue of a special "mystical fluid" imparted to bishops at their consecration, but by virtue of their representing the unity of the Church.

Is the episcopal ministry—whatever name be given it—necessary for the fulness of the life of the Church? It is the answer to this question that actually divides the Churches on the subject of the ministry. And that is why it is of capital importance, if we are to make headway towards the visible unity of the Church, to face this question squarely and attempt to frame an answer to it upon which all can agree. But, to prepare the ground, it is important to define exactly what the episcopal ministry is, and in what its necessity consists. "Catholic" Christians must not, in fact, overburden the notion of this ministry too heavily with all sorts of accessory importances and privileges, due more to history than to ecclesiology properly speaking.

In reading the Acts and the Epistles, we can see quite clearly that a local Church's unity, in itself and with the other Churches in the world, is not simply a grace to rejoice over when it is given, but also a state of obedience to be maintained through prayer. "So that the world believe," all the Churches must display a plainly visible sign of their unity. The Church's mission and its unity are closely connected. Furthermore, the knowledge of the whole of Christian truth is conditioned by unity. Without the charity which visible unity underpins, the light to understand all truth is simply not given. When Christians are divided they tend to run off in various directions with scraps of the truth, and then proceed to inflate them by means of controversy. And the upshot of this is that intractably contradictory notions are manufactured out of conceptions that originally dovetailed one with another.

The apostles worked indefatigably to keep the local Churches in communion with one another in charity, for the sake of fulness in the knowledge of the truth, so that the Church's mission would produce its intended effect. Unity, charity, truth, mission—these are mutual coefficients in the Church; and it is a part of the apostolic ministry to make these coefficients function harmoniously.

We note in the pastoral epistles how much the Apostle is concerned that the "deposit" of faith be "kept." If the Church was to continue to exist, it was necessary that the apostolic office, in its function of guardian of the deposit of faith, be also continued in some way. Of course, the apostles are unique in the history of the Church; but here we find St. Paul seeking to have a ministry of unity, guardian of the sound deposit of faith, be continued, so that the Church could remain in truth and charity for the sake of its mission. The office of Timothy, and that of Titus, made their appearance as something new in the primitive Church, yet implied in the apostolic ministry: Timothy and Titus were charged, as were the apostles, with watching over the visible unity of the local Church, in itself and with other Churches, precisely through the "keeping" of the original deposit of faith.

This ministry—which from this point on we shall call, for the sake of convenience, "episcopal," though without burdening the term with all the accretions of history—is not primarily one of ruling, teaching, or administering the sacraments. It is not the "bishop's" first task to command, or even to govern, like some general or chief of state. The command or rule of the Church he can share with others in a council. Nor is it his essential duty to explain and defend doctrine; this task can be deputed to others —doctors of the Church, and theologians. Nor is he the necessary minister of certain privileged sacraments. It was the will of the Church (acting in harmony with biblical practice) that came into play here, assigning, for example, ordination or confirmation to the bishop because these ecclesiastical acts had a direct relation with the unity of the Church body.

The "episcopal ministry," conceived as the continuation of the apostolic design, is essentially the pastoral ministry of the Word and of the sacraments as these are ordained towards unity through charity for a greater fulness of truth, which are the real object of the Church's mission. The bishop is the minister of unity within the local Church itself, and of the local Church's ecumenical unity; he manifests the presence of the universal Church in the local Church, and of the local Church in the universal, ecumenical, conciliar Church. Of his functions, that is the essential one.

To exercise it, he must sometimes subject others to authority, must "safeguard the deposit of faith," must "ordain" ministers; but these acts, while they do proclaim his essential office—the ministry of unity—do not necessarily belong to him alone, for he can perform them in co-operation with other ministers and can even delegate others to perform them. But the apostolic ministry of unity is intrusted to him personally. A theologian, for example, by his intellectual vigor, or a saint, perhaps, by his personal influence, may abet local unity; still, if this unity is not integrated into ecumenical unity, it can itself become divisive. It is up to the bishop to put local Church unity in accord with universal Church unity.

It seems certain that the solution to the ecumenical problem will consist in the harmonious unity of the two forms of government: episcopal and synodal. The bishop's council should be as representative as possible, and take the form of an annual synod, with pastors and laymen sent as delegates (one pastor and one layman per parish, for example). The bishop would seek the advice of the synod on every question of importance. For questions of lesser moment, he would have the benefit of a permanent synodal council, and on all questions of mere details, he could act alone on his personal responsibility, though ready to render an accounting to the synod. But in any case, in an episcopal-synodal Church, the final responsibility for unity within the local Church and with the universal Church must rest with the bishop, accountable therein to an ecumenical council—and to his Lord.

The quest for visible Church unity involves a very careful scrutiny of the episcopal ministry on the part of "Catholics," so that they may disburden it of all its heavy, non-theological monarchism and enrich it with a thoroughgoing synodal setting; and on the part of "Evangelicals," so that they may disburden their synodal structures of all their heavy scaffolding of democratism, and give them effective point by the admission of a profoundly spiritual ministry of unity.

The ecumenical role of the episcopal ministry is as important as its local role. The office of the bishop involves his constantly cementing the bonds between his Church and the universal Church, both by means of his contacts outside his Church, and by his efforts to endow minds and hearts in the local Church with the ecumenical spirit. The bishops of now separated faiths are already in a position to accomplish this mission; and so, in fact, are certain ecumenical commissions in synodal Churches. But it is clearly the existence of the World Council of Churches, in its interim role of para-conciliar body, which is responsible for fostering this ministry of unity, by bringing together local Church authorities and inspiring in them the quest for visible unity.

If the "Catholic" Churches can claim to possess *de jure* fulness of episcopal functions, there is no doubt that the World Council is preparing the restoration of that fulness *de facto,* that is, the restoration in each Church of an ecumenical ministry, whatever form or name it assume. One may venture to say, in fact, that a "Catholic" bishop has this office of ecumenical unity in his Church, but that if his Church and he himself neither care to nor can enter into some vital relationship with the other Churches, then this office has not reached full exercise. In contrast, thanks to the World Council, the various ministries of unity, or bishops, are even now *de facto* in contact and witnessing the enrichment and invigoration of their function, while awaiting the day when full intercommunion of local Churches will make a full-blown world council possible.

The episcopal ministry of unity serves to exclude an exaggerated centralization of the universal Church. Of course, in a conciliar ecumenical Church, permanent central organs are quite necessary to assure continuity of council undertakings and of inter-Church relations. But the bishops must enjoy great liberty, each in his local Church, a liberty the sole limit upon which is visible communion with the other local Churches. It is thus not a question of their receiving outside orders for application in their Churches, but rather of conforming themselves to conciliar unity through personal meetings and other contacts on the national or world level.

It appears that in a very workable way the Church of the first centuries did realize this ecumenical bond among bishops, who, in turn, remained quite free within their own Churches. Their unity could even become strained, as instanced by the disagreement between Cyprian, bishop of Carthage, and Stephen, bishop of Rome, on the question of rebaptism of heretics. Cyprian recognized the primacy of the bishop of Rome, but was not thereby prevented from standing up to him. The incident shows us both what liberty the local bishops possessed, and at the same time how anxious they were about their ecumenical relationship.

This ecumenical relationship—to return to a consideration of our own day—will obviously require a meeting in council whenever a need to solidify Church unity becomes evident. This relationship also involves, then, the council's possessing a certain authority. What the local ministers of unity, or bishops, accompanied by two or three delegates (theologians and laymen), decide in ecumenical council will take precedence, of course, over any contrary local decisions. The truth appears more clearly in conciliar unity than in local unity. Furthermore, it is quite right that permanent council organs foster and sustain unity and friendly relations among local Churches. For the time being, the World Council of Churches is accomplishing a part of this task, *de facto* if not *de jure*.

It is beyond the scope of our present study to consider the merits of the case for a council primate, who would have power—in order to prevent schism in cases of crisis—to arbitrate questions definitively. We need only direct attention to one point:

The Western church very quickly acknowledged the primacy, *de facto* and *de jure,* of the Church of Rome and of its bishop. The difficulties inherent in relationships among the Churches made necessary the existence of a model Church, a pattern of unity, a master copy, as it were, to which the other Churches could refer in order to insure their communion one with another. Theological reasons—the primacy of Peter over the other apostles—played a great part in this, but certainly the necessity of union among local Churches, and of a model Church to which these could conform in order to avoid schism and heresy, played an equally important part. The local Church of Rome and its bishop were placed before other local Churches and other bishops so that these might have in view an ideal of the Church, an ideal of a bishop, an ideal of Church unity, which besides inspiring and inspiriting them would insure their uniformity by providing them all with the same pattern.

And we find the early Church very insistent upon the Roman Church's actually fulfilling its function as model Church, and the Roman bishop's discharging his office as model bishop. This perhaps explains certain strains, certain harshnesses, to which the bishop of Rome was submitted—as in the just-cited case of Cyprian, who was not calling into doubt the primacy of Peter, and of the pope, but was importuning the bishop and the Church of Rome to provide him with a solution—which he wanted to be the same as *his* solution—to his vexing problem.

But for Rome to have the primacy it had to have also the fulness of Church life. The primitive local Churches looked to Rome not only because they saw in it the Church of the Prince of the Apostles, but because they saw in it the Church of the martyrs, of Peter, of Paul, and of the long list of others, the living Church, the exemplary Church, the mother of missionaries and of martyrs.

They found in the bishop of Rome a bishop indeed, watchful over his flock, over his local Church, and exercising therein the fulness of the apostolic ministry. When, today, we witness the progressive revival of this conception of the bishop of Rome as real shepherd of his local Church—in the person of John XXIII, who uses his local episcopal office as an angle from which to ascertain the needs of the Church and of the world, and has determined to be the very pattern of a bishop in the pattern of a Church—do we not have grounds for hope of major developments in the Roman Catholic Church? When the local Church of Rome will have become once again a living Church both for itself and for others, the head of a universal, biblical, liturgical revival, deeply solicitous over direct contact with the world, with all its sufferings and its yearnings, really the Church of the poor, of the hungry for bread and for justice, the Church of the martyrs, then, perhaps, we shall better understand what that Church must have been for the other local Churches in the early centuries.

Equipped with ample information and communications facilities, the World Council of Churches today can act as a clearing house to make illuminating experiences in various parts of the world available to all local Churches. Thus, for example, the Church of South India has supplied the pattern of a Church whose overwhelming concern for unity is dictated by the needs of the Church's mission, and has stimulated other local Churches to look into the possibility of union among themselves. For the role of pattern for local Churches can be played successively by various Churches (whenever the Holy Ghost breathes there) and can be brought to our attention through the ecumenical relations afforded by the World Council.

The rediscovery, by the synodal Churches, of the ministry of unity, and the profounder appreciation of this ministry on the part of the episcopal Churches would be an important step towards local Churches' mutual recognition and possible exchange of one another's ministers—the next to final sign of full unity. For such mutual recognition and possible exchange to become a reality, certain very exact specifications would still have to be met:

For example, the "Catholic" Churches will have to define, and to explore further, their position as regards a minister who has not been ordained by a bishop—such a minister as found in the synodal Churches. What is their understanding of the call and of the ministry of a pastor not ordained by a bishop? And the "Evangelical" Churches will have to look into the possibility of fitting into the structure of their organizations the ministry of unity—the episcopal ministry—which, since it is, after all, the ecumenical bond with other Churches, might be entrusted to men consecrated by a number of bishops representing various different local Churches which already possess this ministry. Now on neither side need this be a renunciation of proper values. It could rather be an ecumenical expansion for missionary ends—proof of which is to be found in the Church of South India today. For "theological sacrifices" in this direction constitute, not renouncements, but fruitions.

We deliberately avoid treating here of the problem of apostolic succession. One thing is certain: this problem has not received sufficient study; and the "Catholic" Churches are called upon for an enormous effort at clarifying what their requirements for real succession are. In any case, one may wonder whether apostolic succession is not a matter which can be understood, after all, only from the inside—whether it is not more of an ecclesiastical fact than an ecclesiological doctrine. However this may be, it is too early to present the problem before the "Catholic" Churches and the "Evangelical" Churches have really learned to live together on some terms, borrowing from each other certain forms of ministry which they are bound to find an enrichment: the "Catholic" Churches in providing larger scope for the synod and for the laity, and the "Evangelical" Churches in making the experiment of embodying the ministry of unity—the episcopate—in their organization.

3) *Intercommunion.*

Sacramental intercommunion will constitute the final realization of visible unity. In fact, when the Churches are able to exchange ministers and to participate together in the same Eucharist, then problems of organization, liturgical differences, various non-theological differentiating factors—these will no longer constitute any real division. Universal visible unity will be fully realized amidst the variety of local traditions.

Yes, eucharistic intercommunion will be the end of ecumenical labors; it will be visible unity come true.

Certain Churches, in the category we have been identifying as "Catholic," are very strict on the matter of admitting others to their communion, and of allowing their own to communicate outside their Church. In this, they are being consistent with their conception of the Church, and with both their teaching on Christian initiation and their teaching on ordination and the apostolic succession. Only a Christian baptized and instructed—even confirmed—in that Church may be a regular communicant therein; conversely, he may not receive communion from a minister who has not been ordained in the apostolic succession. This strict and coherent position is consistent in its intransigence; but, in emphasizing almost exclusively the ecclesiastical character of eucharistic communion, it may make communion seem, not at all the cause, but strictly the result of unity.

Other Churches, in the category we have been identifying as "Evangelical," consider the Sacred Banquet as an activity of Christ's in his Church. He issues invitations to those who belong to him (and who these are he alone knows). Christ gives himself to anyone he pleases. Christ himself gathers his Church together in the Sacred Banquet, and there forges it into a unity. This notion, which leads to an invitation-at-large, welcoming any and all of the baptized to the communion table, an "open communion," emphasizes almost exclusively Christ's initiative in the sacrament. The danger here is that any sense of sound Church discipline, with exclusion of "unworthy" communions, will be lost, worthiness to communiate being left entirely a matter of self-scrutiny, save in the case of public sinners, where excommunication becomes operative.

Each of the two preceding positions contains a great share of truth, and yet it is difficult to see how to reconcile them. Perhaps on both sides a more careful study should be made of the part played in eucharistic communion by unity—both as cause and as result. Of course, the sacrament of unity par excellence cannot be turned into a sham to camouflage significant disagreements; yet, on the other hand, if Christ is really present, and really received in this sacrament, is there not in it a power for ecumenical union which ought to be utilized?

The solution perhaps lies in profiting by such occasions for intercommunion as ecumenical gatherings, where it may be assumed that each communicant is theologically enlightened enough to interpret this intercommunion as a act of faith in Christ's desire to unify his Church through the Eucharist, and not as a gesture of indifferentism.

The Eucharist, then, plays the same part in the framework of the ecumenical movement as it plays in any particular Church, where, as we know, not all Christians are necessarily in agreement on every point, yet are brought into relationship, gathered together, and fused into a single body by the Body of Christ, really present.

Churches which theologically and devotionally are unable to practice intercommunion must be respected in their faithfulness to their convictions and in their doctrinal consistency. Churches, in contrast, which can with clear conscience practice this intercommunion should do so unabashedly, certain that Christ will thereby unify them ever more closely. But let them then conduct themselves consistently with their act of visible unity. How—if they agree to be united thus visibly in one body, through one and the same communion—can they continue to think of themselves as divided? How can, say, a Lutheran Church and a Calvinist Church, when they are in full intercommunion and even practicing an exchange of ministers, continue to put stock in their division? Even if, for practical reasons, they must go on keeping up separate organizations, they ought to announce their visible unity as an accomplished fact. Otherwise, either they are unaware of what they are doing in practicing intercommunion, or else they are using intercommunion to dissimulate irreconcilable differences, that is, making the sacrament of unity an out-and-out sham.

No, two Churches welcoming each other's communicants and sending ministers to each other must think of themselves as visibly one, though each with its own theological, liturgical, and practical traditions, to be preserved as an enrichment of their unity. They must admit that their continued separation into two distinct organisms is ecclesiologically meaningless, and that if they make no attempt to merge, they are attaching greater importance to non-theological factors than to the efficacious sign of unity bestowed in the Sacred Banquet.

Besides, the fact is that the practice of intercommunion between Calvinists and Lutherans has brought them closer together than they sometimes think, and their unity today is more real than ever before. (But at the same time, let them not allow themselves to be befogged by a conception of unity which would be rather a centralizing uniformity than a living union of local Churches such as the New Testament and the early centuries displayed.) Since they practice full intercommunion, these Churches are in the stage of visible unity. All that is left for them to do is to merge their organizations, so that for every single place there will be a corresponding single Church of the Gospel. Of course, there will still remain some other Churches in the same territory; but the inclusiveness characteristic of this Church of the Gospel will be a standing reminder that this heterogeneity is abnormal, and that total unity, in a single local Church in communion with the universal Church, should be an object of daily prayer and daily effort. But even now let those who share one single Eucharist realize the implications of the fact, believing that they have already achieved everything necessary for them to consider themselves a single visible local Church!

No ecclesiastical structure, however strong it may be, is a guarantee of visible unity. We have only to think of the sixteenth-century Reform. Even the organization of the Roman Church, and papal authority, were not enough to insure the visible unity of the Church in the West. If the Holy Spirit be not constantly invoked—and obeyed—visibly unity is in danger of dissolution, because of human differences, and because of sin.

Thus, when a local Church has recovered full visible unity through fusion of various traditions, and when the universal Church has recovered its conciliar unity, ecumenical labors will still not be really completed. There still will be meetings to be arranged, other contacts to be established, exchanges to be maintained, so that local Churches do not fall into isolation and thus endanger unity. Most of all will it be necessary for the Church to live in the light and the charity of the Holy Spirit, and to be constantly renewed and enlivened by him. It must always be being led towards the wholeness of truth. And this truth is not a static dogmatic system, but a living reality, progressively more conscious of itself, deepening, unfolding, enriching itself in pace with the history of which it is a part. Not that truth changes, but its implications are better and better realized by virtue of the ever-fresh reading of the Scriptures accomplished by the ecumenical Church in its vital contacts with the modern world.

The Church must ask the Holy Spirit to sanctify it both in its members and in its authorities. The Church is holy by virtue of the Gospel it proclaims and the sacraments it administers, because God himself is present in these acts. But, at the same time, the Church is made up of sinful men, and must never tire of calling them unto sanctification in the Holy Spirit.

This sanctification—without which unity will simply not be maintained—must be evidenced by the spirit of sacrifice. Unity requires that the individual, the group, and the local Church agree to sacrifice themselves for the good of the catholicity of the Church. Without this spirit of sacrifice for the sake of unity, individualist and sectarian interests will soon gain the upper hand over universality. Visible unity, a condition for fulness of charity and truth and for the efficaciousness of the Church's mission, must be regarded as a gift so precious that much must be willingly sacrificed for the sake of keeping it from strain and from downright rupture.

The Church must be ever reimmersed in the spirit of Christ's priestly prayer (John 17) in order to revive within itself the holiness and spirit of sacrifice called for by visible unity and an efficacious mission. Christ sacrificed himself in order that all might be one, and that the world might believe; the Church, his Body, can do no better than to follow in his footsteps, and to call constantly upon the Holy Spirit to sanctify it by the spirit of sacrifice, so that it may always preserve visible unity and so that the world may believe that Jesus Christ is Lord of the Church and of the world.

Tradition

2 Tradition

In ecumenical discussions, the problem of tradition is among those that reappear most frequently. One of the four commissions of the theological department of the World Council of Churches—Faith and Constitution—is devoting its research to "Tradition and Traditions."[1] Exegetical and historical studies during the past decades have doubtless considerably altered the appearance of the problem.[2]

It is plain to be seen that the long-standing attitude of Protestant apologetics no longer holds—namely, that the Church must

[1] See the Documents of this commission, in particular the following:
S. L. Greenslade, *The Formation of the New Testament Canon, Motives and Principles,* paper for the Theological Commission on Tradition and Traditions (Faith and Order), 1956; D. W. Hay, *Scriptures and the Tradition, idem,* 1957; A. C. Outler, *The Sense of Tradition in the Ante-Nicene Church, idem,* 1957; K. Bonis, *Kirche und Heiliger Geist in orthodoxer Sicht, idem,* 1958; J.-L. Leuba, "Le rapport entre l'Esprit et la tradition selon le Nouveau Testament," *Verbum Caro,* L (1959), 151–170; A. C. Moore, *Tradition and the New Testament Canon,* 1959; K. E. Skydsgaard, *Interim Report of the Theological Commission on Tradition and Traditions,* 1960; J. Pelikan, *Overcoming History by History,* 1960. These documents are available at the World Council of Churches, 17 route de Malagnou, Geneva.

[2] See the good bibliography on the problem of tradition, comprising over two hundred titles for the years 1930 to 1960, prepared by G. Pedersen for the Theological Commission on Tradition and Traditions (Faith and Order), and two recent volumes: H. Holstein, *La tradition dans l'Eglise,* Paris: Grasset, 1960, and Y. M.-J. Congar, *La tradition et les traditions, essai historique,* Paris: Arthème Fayard, 1960.

base the whole of its teaching on the Bible alone, everything added by the tradition of men being useless, or even dangerous to the purity of the Gospel. This position, which was that neither of the Reformers nor of the theologians of the seventeenth century, but appeared with various spiritual movements in the nineteenth century, is today entirely out of date.[3]

The Church is again conceived of as the holy and visible Body of Christ; and what goes on in it—in its life and its thought, in its liturgy and its dogmas—is neither insignificant, useless, nor dangerous. Tradition is inevitable, and is necessary for the total understanding of the truth.

It is no less plain to be seen that the attitude of classical Catholic apologetics is no longer in force, either—namely, that tradition is a second source of Revelation, that it is parallel in rank with the Scriptures, or that Scripture is but an accident in the history of the Church, founded in the first place upon an oral tradition; that tradition preceded the Scriptures, that since it was the Church that determined what was Scripture and what was not, the authority of the Church is above the authority of the Scriptures, and that tradition fills in items omitted from the Scriptures.

Any confrontation of the former positions of the two sides would be, of course, fruitless.

True enough, Christ did found a Church; he himself wrote nothing; he made no arrangements for a Scripture. This Church of Christ's designated a Scripture—composed of apostolic documents—without excluding an authorized interpretation of these documents, an authentic tradition preserving their true sense. But it is at this point that there arises the problem of the relationship between the Scriptures and tradition, between revelation and the life of the Church—in its custody of the deposit of faith, in its liturgy, and in its missionary undertakings.

Tradition may be considered from three different complementary viewpoints:

as the life of the Gospel in the Church,
as the act by which the Church transmits the Gospel,
as the product of this life and this act.

[3] PELIKAN, *op.cit.*

TRADITION, LIFE OF THE GOSPEL IN THE CHURCH

Christ, the Son of God, God himself made flesh, came at a certain point in time to bring to Israel the Gospel of salvation for the whole world. By his life, his words, his deeds, by his death and resurrection, he transmitted to his apostles, to his disciples, to those who customarily accompanied him, God's very truth. This Word of God, living in the form of a man, was heard, was seen, was grasped—by men. "Our message concerns that Word, who is life," says St. John (1 John 1:1–3), "what he was from the first, what we have heard about him, what our own eyes have seen of him; what it was that met our gaze, and the touch of our hands. Yes, life dawned; and it is as eye-witnesses that we give you the news of that life, that eternal life, which ever abode with the Father and has dawned, now, upon us. This message about what we have seen and heard we pass on to you, so that you, too, may share in our fellowship."

It was with the fulness of their individual human personalities that his apostles, his disciples, his other contemporaries heard, saw, and understood the human-divine personality of Christ. The truth—which he both embodied and spoke of—made its impression on different intelligences, different psychologies, among them. Their memories were stamped, their wills attracted, their imaginations stirred, all differently. According to their characters or their temperaments, different images arose in their minds as they heard the Master speak. John the contemplative and Peter the impetuous heard the same word, saw the same miracle, but with different eyes, and minds, and hearts. The variety—in unity—we find in the reports furnished by the four gospels is clear proof of this difference in perception—at the same time as it is a striking proof of authenticity.

Thus, from its first proclamation by Christ himself, the Gospel—which was not immediately taken down as though by some stenographer—began to live in the personal consciousness of each hearer. Moreover, Christ spoke to the Twelve, to groups of various sizes, and to large crowds; and thus collective reaction also played a part in the variety of impressions made by the Gospel. In accordance with the different kinds of questions asked as well as with the different kinds of reactions in different audiences, the Word of Christ was tinged by each collective consciousness which received it. Each individual and each group belonged to one or another of the spiritual traditions which made up the Judaism of that day. Each particular religious tradition lent its own hue to the understanding of the words of Christ. Thus his words could be understood predominantly legalistically, or ascetically, or mystically, or elastically, or nationalistically, or cosmopolitanly, or Judaistically, or Hellenistically, or monastically, or socially . . .

God, in planning the incarnation at a particular time, in the particular location of Israel, foresaw these human reactions as making up the inevitable and indeed indispensable exterior side of revelation. The Gospel was not something to drop from the sky, complete with leather binding and gold edges; it had first to exist as life—in the human nature of Christ—and then to be transmitted under the conditions of human life, to concrete individual human beings.

But was not the Word of God, transmitted to men under the conditions just described, in danger of being misunderstood, or modified, or even falsified, if the impression it produced could be affected by the so different natures of the individuals who received it? No, the unity of testimony furnished by the four different gospels despite their diversity is proof enough that God had provided for an agent and an organization to maintain the truth of revelation in its essential purity.

Christ, in choosing twelve apostles as eyewitnesses of his life, death, and resurrection, in sending them out as his envoys, just as he had been sent as the envoy of the Father, and in giving them the Holy Spirit, who would recall to their minds everything he had said to them and would lead them into all truth (John 14:26; 16:13), took effective steps against any deterioration of the Gospel, providing for an agent and an organization for the faithful transmission of his Word.[4]

The agent for the authentic tradition of revelation was the Holy Spirit, and the organization for giving it expression was the

[4] J.-Cl. Margot, "L'apostolat dans le Nouveau Testament et la succession apostolique," *Verbum Caro,* XLIII (1957), 213–225.

apostolate.[5] The Gospel was not abandoned to the hazards of a multiple human understanding; the Holy Spirit was to revive the authentic Word of Christ in the memories of the apostles, and was to lead them into all truth. They were thus assured of the infallible assistance of the Holy Spirit, and were made successors of Christ in the faithful transmission of the Word of God.

The life of the Gospel in the original Church, constituted by the college of apostles, was therefore directed and controlled by the Holy Spirit, poured out upon them at Pentecost. Now Pentecost was not the first act of a new era after a termination, at the ascension, of the era of the incarnation. Rather, it was the final act in the history of salvation wrought by the incarnation of the Son of God. By the sending of the Holy Spirit, Christ, the High Priest, having entered into the holy of holies, consecrated his apostles in their unique and definitive function of "ministers plenipotentiary."

They were commissioned, with all the power of Christ and of the Spirit, to extend the Church to the very ends of the earth. Their word would be the very Word of the Father and the Son, recalled to their minds by the Holy Spirit. Christ had said to them, before his ascension, "All authority in heaven and on earth has been given to me; you, *therefore,* must go out, making disciples of all nations, and baptizing them in the name of the Father, and of the Son, and of the Holy Spirit, teaching them to observe all the commandments which I have given you. And behold I am with you all through the days that are coming, until the consummation of the world" (Matt. 28:18–20). These words had been addressed essentially to the Twelve (their number soon to be recompleted by Matthias). Christ possessed all power; and, in virtue of this power, he sent them as the Father had sent him. They were to extend the Church to all nations by means of baptism and the preaching of the Gospel. To do so, they would have the power of Christ and the light of the Holy Spirit. Christ would be with them to the end of the world. The apostles would never be separated from Christ; he and they would be one in this worldwide mission, until his return—which they thought of as imminent,

[5] J. Colson, *Les fonctions ecclésiales aux deux premiers siècles* (Paris: Desclée de Brouwer, 1956), pp. 11–32.

because of the mystery of the day and the hour kept privy by the Father.

Pentecost, then, was their consecration by the Holy Spirit as ministers of Christ, invested with all his power, and insured of his constant presence. Thanks to the Holy Spirit, Christ and they were one in their world-wide mission and in their founding of Churches. Their word was his Word. They were transmitters of revelation; they imparted truth; and this they did in the light of the Holy Spirit, who illuminated them, and by the power of Christ, who assisted them.

The Gospel, which they were to carry to the four corners of the world, would in them be preserved, therefore, in its purity by the light of the Holy Spirit. Granted, they had received that Gospel in accordance with the different human makeup of each, their differently stamped personalities, their own understandings, their own psychologies; but the Holy Spirit, who was to recall it to their minds, was to lead them into all truth. The Gospel would have its existence in them, and in their transmission of it; but neither this individualized existence nor this transmission would jeopardize the truth, for it was the Holy Spirit who would produce that existence and direct that tradition so that the Gospel would continue in its purity.

The Holy Spirit had been promised to the apostles by Christ—who had invested them with his power—as insurance for a living and faithful tradition of the Gospel. The Holy Spirit, as agent of the living and faithful transmission of the truth, would inspire and assist the apostles in their ministry, for they were the organization for this transmission. But still another essential factor in this faithfulness of transmission was the collegiate nature of the apostolate.

Christ had not provided himself with *one* successor, nor with *individual* successors. He promised his presence and his assistance to a group of men. (One must not, by the way, think of the Church as something which succeeded Christ upon his retirement. The Ascension was no withdrawal on Christ's part, but simply a change in the form of his activity. From then on, Christ was to act invisibly through the medium of the apostolate and the Church, but it was always to be he who was present and acting. The apostolate, invested with his authority, filled with his power, inspired and assisted by the Holy Spirit, was to be the sign and the instrument of Christ ever living, present, and acting in the world.)

Now, the apostolate was a college, composed in the first instance of the Twelve, chosen by Christ (Judas was to be replaced by Matthias). And this collegiality is very important for an understanding of their ministry. The fact that the apostles were different men, yet made up a society, engaging in mutual relationships, was a guarantee of the plenitude of their ministry. They were commissioned to transmit—together—a single Gospel, of which each of them would particularly emphasize one or more features. Thus they would complete one another, they would be complementary parts, in their collegiate testimony. The collegiality of the apostolate gives evidence of the humility of their ministry: invested with the authority of Christ and with the vigor of the Spirit, the apostolate remained the sign and servant of Christ, the proclaimer of the Word and directing power in the Church. It was not an apostle who governed the Church of Christ by himself, but Christ acting through the apostolic college. The collegiality of the apostolate gives evidence also of the solidarity of the apostles' ministry: their transmission of the Gospel and government of the Church was a common one. This solidarity was a guarantee of theological balance: all spiritual and psychological tendencies were united in the apostolic college.

Thus—through the power of Christ, the inspiration of the Holy Spirit, and the collegiate nature of the apostolate—the Gospel would be preserved from alteration in its career in the Church, and its transmission would take place authoritively, insuring original purity and totality. Christ's power, residing in his apostles, gave them full authority in the transmission of the word of God; the inspiration of the Holy Spirit insured the essential purity of the Gospel as possessed and transmitted by them; the collegiate nature of the apostolate kept them in possession of all the richness, variety, and universality, as well as of the unity, of revelation.

This collegiality, guarantee of catholicity in the understanding and transmission of the Gospel, was not an undifferentiated one; certain apostles played a primary part in it: first Peter, then James and John, then Paul.[6]

[6] O. CULLMANN, *Saint Pierre, disciple, apôtre, martyr,* Neuchâtel and Paris: Delachaux et Niestlé, 1950.

TRADITION, ACT BY WHICH THE CHURCH TRANSMITS THE GOSPEL

The apostles were not primarily commissioned to transmit a document recording Christ's words, deeds, and actions. At any rate, nothing in the New Testament can be the basis for the idea that Christ gave them that precise task. Christ founded the apostolate, and gave it all power, assuring it of his constant presence and the assistance of the Holy Spirit. The apostolate was primarily a group of men, chosen, consecrated, provided with divine assistance, commissioned to transmit it the Gospel of Christ. This they were to do with all their human resources, assisted by the Holy Spirit. This transmission was to be a living one, based upon a divinely assisted memory, the product of divinely guided reflection, the echo of a personal understanding, stamped with a particular psychology. This combination of the Holy Spirit's direction and of personal testimony was to give to the apostolic ministry of each apostle its characteristic and living style. They were to proclaim the one and only divine truth, each according to the individuality of his human personality. The transmission spoken of—or tradition—would therefore be a living thing, a human thing, yet it would be the transmission or tradition of the one and the same Gospel of Christ.[7]

Invested with Christ's power, and inspired by the Holy Spirit, the apostles were to assume all the responsibilities of their commission, in the liberty permitted them by that power and inspiration. Thus it was that some of them—without giving up the oral tradition of the Gospel—wrote down those words, deeds, and actions of Christ which were soon to constitute the gospels. Others wrote epistles in which they epitomized their teaching (in turn a faithful echo of Christ's teaching). This written transmission was a common-sense procedure on the part of the apostles, desirous of communicating Christ's history and Christ's words exactly, so that their hearers—who were neither eyewitnesses, nor chosen by

[7] O. CULLMANN, *La tradition, problème exégétique, historique et apologétique* (Cahiers théologiques 33), Neuchâtel and Paris: Delachaux et Niestlé, 1953; see the recent discussion in HOLSTEIN, pp. 249 ff.

the Lord, nor invested with his power, nor inspired by the Holy Spirit—would not be in danger of misunderstanding or of distorting a solely oral tradition.

Besides this, it is quite understandable that men reared in the Jewish tradition, where the Sacred Writings of the Old Testament enjoyed so great authority, should have been quickly led to preserve the treasure of Christ's Gospel in written form. It was not their original intention to add their writings to the canonical books of the Old Testament; yet they did intend to show how these reached their fulfilment and full significance in Jesus Christ.

The writings that make up the New Testament were not, then, an accident occurring in the course of a transmission that might have remained purely oral. It was humanly and spiritually necessary for the oral tradition to become a written tradition. Humanly prompted, yet directed by the Holy Spirit, and with all the authority of Christ, certain sacred writers, either eyewitnesses of the events narrated or disciples of the apostles, fixed in written form—with the assistance of the Holy Spirit—the apostolic memoirs, with a view to accurate retransmission on the part of those who, not having known Christ, and not having, as apostles, been invested with his authority, might have distorted the one and only Gospel.

The apostles first believed in the early return of Christ; for God alone had possession of the secret of that day and that hour. And this belief considerably—and providentially—affected the conception they formed of the transmission of the Gospel.

Instituted as a college of twelve (symbol of the new Israel; the old had had twelve patriarchs and twelve tribes), familiar associates of Christ from the time of his baptism until his ascension, eyewitnesses of his resurrection, envoys of their Lord (the envoy of the Father), sent to be the organs of transmission of the Gospel and of the Spirit, and the guardians of the unity of the Church, these apostles—with the power of Christ and the inspiration of the Holy Spirit—were to be the foundation upon which God would build his Church. United with Christ, who was to be with them until the end of the world, they had full power to transmit the Gospel and the Holy Spirit, and to gather together the people of God.

Yet Christ had not placed them alone in the office of the

ministry. Their place was unique, and unalienable; but the Lord had also sent the seventy disciples (or seventy-two, in certain manuscripts) to proclaim the Good News (Luke 10:1–16). As the twelve apostles were the image of the twelve patriarchs, the seventy disciples were the image of the seventy elders appointed by Moses to share his duties (Num. 11:16–17, 24–29; with Eldad and Medad, they numbered seventy two). These, too, were invested with an authority such as prompted Christ to say: "He who listens to you, listens to me; he who despises you, despises me; and he who despises me, despises him that sent me" (Luke 10:16). Without being the foundations of the Church, as were the twelve apostles, the seventy disciples were still ministers of Christ, invested with his authority, sent to proclaim the Gospel of salvation.[8]

Very soon the twelve apostles themselves, following the example of Christ, were to commission still other Christians with certain responsibilities of the ministry. Yet even before this the glorified Christ himself, always acting with them, had created other apostles. He had put Matthias in the place of Judas, by revealing his choice through the Twelve's drawing of lots (Acts 1:23–26). He had even added a thirteenth apostle, when he appeared to Saul of Tarsus in a vision. Paul thereupon became an eyewitness of the resurrection, commissioned and sent out by the glorified Christ himself. The Lord had thus broken the restricted circle of the Twelve, as if to invite them to widen the apostolate. Others bore the title of apostle, and Christ revealed himself to them (1 Cor. 15:7). Still others, who perhaps had not seen the risen Christ, had been called and had been created apostles through the intermediary of the Twelve or of St. Paul (Gal. 1:1); Barnabas (Acts 14:14), Andronicus and Junias (Rom. 16:17), and Silvanus (1 Thess. 2:7).

Still others, "companions in the labors" of St. Paul, seem to have exercised a veritable apostolic ministry: Titus (2 Cor. 8:23), Epaphroditus (Philip. 2:25), Timothy (1 Thess. 1:1; 2 Thess. 1:1), and perhaps others still (Col. 4:10 ff.). These were apostolic collaborators or auxiliary apostles.

[8] R. PAQIER, "L'épiscopat dans la structure institutionelle de l'Eglise," *Verbum Caro,* XLIX (1959), 32.

By appearing to Saul of Tarsus, the Lord had revealed to the twelve apostles the possibility of the extension of the original college because of its universal mission and of the numerous responsibilities in store.[9] Of course, the Twelve and St. Paul retained in the Church a unique and unalienable authority and station; but they could share their commission and could appoint men who, under their control, would exercise an apostolic mission. Since they possessed the power of Christ and the inspiration of the Holy Ghost, and since the Lord had shown them the way by adding Paul to their number, the apostles were at liberty to extend the apostolate in accordance with the requirements of their mission and of their ministry.

So, besides the new apostles, the Twelve and St. Paul were to create various kinds of ministers for the service of the Gospel and of the Church. They appointed the Seven at Jerusalem to minister to Greek-speaking Christians (Acts 6:1–7). We find presbyters appearing in Jerusalem, with James, the brother of the Lord, taking his place among them as a bishop (Acts 11:30; 12:17; 15; 21:18). In Churches everywhere St. Paul appointed colleges of presbyters (Acts 14:22; 20:17 ff.), for whom he acted as visiting bishop.

Both by the extension of the visitant apostolate and by the appointment of numerous local ministers, the Twelve and St. Paul, while retaining their unique authority and control, shared their increasingly heavy duties with others. The career of the Gospel in the Churches was thus multiple and diversified, the work of numerous ministers, but always under the principal authority of apostles invested with Christ‘s power and assured of the inspiration of the Holy Spirit. Even the others who were apostles remained directly dependent upon the Twelve and St. Paul.

All these auxiliary ministers were appointed by reason of the geographic extension of the Church; but the apostles, who were looking for the return of the Christ, gave no thought to a succession in time. Their idea was to extend the apostolic college somewhat by adding some new apostles to their number, while

[9] J.-L. LEUBA, *L'institution et l'événement,* Neuchâtel and Paris: Delachaux et Niestlé, 1950.

themselves fulfilling the episcopal functions of surveillance and unity until the coming of the Lord. If, at Jerusalem, James exercised a local episcopal ministry among a college of presbyters, Paul undertook, and his collaborators undertook, a visitant episcopate of the Churches which he had founded. In some cases, he had appointed ministers grouped in colleges of presbyters without a presiding officer, in others—although this is less certain—he had directed the ministers to assume in turn the role of episcopal presbyter.[10]

But finally, faced with the prospect of death before the return of the Lord, the apostles turned their thoughts to the continuation in time of their ministry as guardians of the deposit of faith and safeguarders of unity. Of course, it was impossible that they should have successors in so far as they were the sole foundations of the Church, chosen by Christ, eyewitnesses of his life, his death, and his resurrection, invested with his power, and assured of the inspiration of the Holy Spirit. Yet, that part of their ministry which consisted in watching over the transmission of the Gospel and the unity of the Church had to be continued; for the authentic deposit of faith had to be preserved in its accuracy, and the Churches' unity in truth and charity maintained.

Thus we find St. Paul intrusting to Timothy and to Titus the guardianship both of the deposit of faith and of unity. Once apostolic collaborators or auxiliary apostles, they now became real successors of the apostles, and would—after the deaths of the Twelve and of Paul himself—continue the duties of the apostles among the various Churches. Theirs it would be to watch over the purity both of doctrine and of Christian conduct, to ordain ministers, presbyters, supervisors (local bishops), and deacons, to preserve local Churches from division, etc. And theirs it would be, furthermore, to provide in turn for successors to themselves.[11]

We may sum up this whole situation thus: Christ chose the apostolate to found—by his authority and the inspiration of the Holy Spirit—his Church; the apostles wrote the history of Christ, and composed letters epitomizing his teaching; now it would not

[10] J.-PH. MENOUD, *L'Eglise et les ministères selon le Nouveau Testament* (Cahiers théologiques 22), Neuchâtel and Paris: Delachaux et Niestlé, 1949.

[11] COLSON, pp. 145–162.

do for their approaching deaths and Christ's delayed return to leave the Churches without guardians of unity and of the treasury of faith. The valid deposit of faith, then, was to be both safeguarded and transmitted by their successors—apostolic delegates whom they now invested with such part of the apostolic authority as could be transmitted to them, namely, this very authority to safeguard the apostolic treasury of faith, to pass it on accurately, and to hold the Church together in unity. Thus, the tradition—or transmission—of the Gospel, in its course from Christ to the apostles, and from the apostles to their apostolic collaborators and to the various ministers they appointed and Churches they founded was to be able to continue after their deaths.

The successors of the apostles, as we have indicated, did not replace the apostles as foundations of the Church. From the apostles their successors received the Gospel; from their hands they had the documents; and to these objective data of the original tradition they could constantly refer. The fidelity of these successors would consist in safeguarding the apostolic treasury of faith and in handing it on conscientiously. Thus the apostles continued their ministry in their successors, and remained forever present in the Church by their word, which was none other than that which they had received from Christ.

But this new transmission, by the apostles' successors, did not consist simply in the reading of the documents which they had now taken in hand. Like the original transmission, it was a living thing, necessarily adapting itself to the exigencies of the Church's life. Now what power and what assistance had these successors of the apostles in the performance of this task? Obviously, they had not the power to continue the work of Christ as foundation stones of the Church (these had been already laid), nor the inspiration of the Holy Spirit to carry out the original transmission of the Gospel (this had been completed). If they founded Churches, they would do so atop the foundations already laid by the apostles; if they transmitted the Gospel, this would be the Gospel which the apostles originally transmitted as they had it from Christ—the Gospel recalled to the apostles memories by the Holy Spirit. Gone now was the freedom possessed by the original apostles by virtue of the power of Christ and the inspiration of the Holy Spirit; the measure of the successors' apostolic power was guardianship and accurate transmission of the valid deposit of apostolic faith.

And yet, they did have fulness of authority. The Apostle wrote to Titus (Tit. 2:15): "Be this thy message, lending all authority to thy encouragement and thy reproof." This authority is that of the apostle himself, always present in his successor by virtue of the treasure of faith which he has transmitted to him; this authority is that of the Holy Spirit, who inspired the apostle, bringing the Gospel of Christ anew to his memory, and who will assist his successor, keeping him faithful to the apostle and, through the latter, to Christ.

The apostolate, an essential necessity to Christ's foundation of the Church, continues its presence in the apostolic successors to effect the accurate transmission of the Gospel. In other words, the apostolic successors are the instruments whereby the apostles transmit the Gospel from generation to generation; the Gospel of the apostles, inspired by the Holy Spirit, remains alive in the Church, and is transmitted faithfully through apostolic successors. The authority of the latter depends upon their fidelity to the apostolic deposit of faith; however, because the Gospel is not simply a book to be republished, but a living Word, a Sacred Scripture to be explained within the communion of the Church, living apostolic successors are necessary to carry on this living transmission of the Gospel, and they are assisted by the Holy Spirit in this transmission.

The successor of an apostle, we repeat, has the Holy Spirit to assist him in this transmission. St. Paul said to Timothy (2 Tim. 1:6): "That is why I would remind thee to fan the flame of that special grace which God kindled in thee, when my hands were laid upon thee." And the Spirit which Titus had received "is not one that shrinks from danger; it is a spirit of action, of love, and of discipline" (2 Tim. 1:7). Titus was thus invested with the authority of the Holy Spirit who was to assist him in his duties as apostolic successor. But this office he could not discharge independently of the apostle or of the apostolate. The apostolate continued to exercise its ministry in the Church: the apostles sat enthroned, judging the new Israel (Matt. 19:28). It was therefore in communion with the apostolate that the apostolic successor could exercise his ministry and continue the faithful transmission of the

Gospel. "Do not blush, then," said Paul to Timothy, "for the witness thou bearest to our Lord, or for me, who am his prisoner; share all the tribulations of the gospel message as God gives thee strength" (2 Tim. 1:8). The successor is to keep to the pattern of sound doctrine which he has learned from the apostle's lips (2 Tim. 1:13).

St. Paul continues: "By the power of the Holy Spirit who dwells in us, be true to thy high trust" (2 Tim. 1:14). Much is suggested in these few words, the development of the implications of which occupies the bulk of the epistles to Timothy and Titus. The apostolic successor must be true to the high trust given the apostles, namely, Christ's Gospel brought to the minds of the apostles by the inspiration of the Holy Spirit. The successors to the apostles have heard this Gospel from the lips of the apostles themselves; moreover this inspired oral tradition has already been transcribed in the written Gospels and apostolic Letters. "Everything in the scripture has been divinely inspired, and has its uses; to instruct us, to expose our errors, to correct our faults, to educate us in holy living; so God's servant will become a master of his craft, and each noble task that comes will find him ready for it" (2 Tim. 3:16). Here the Apostle is certainly alluding to Christian writings. This trust the apostolic successor must safeguard and transmit to others: "Thou hast learned, from many who can witness to it, the doctrine which I hand down; give it into the keeping of men thou canst trust, men who will know how to teach it to others besides themselves" (2 Tim. 2:2). This holding fast to the charge committed, and this transmission of the apostolic Gospel ("Fix thy mind on Jesus Christ, sprung from the race of David, who has risen from the dead; that is the gospel I preach" 2 Tim. 2:8), and not of another gospel, he may accomplish faithfully thanks to the assistance of the Holy Spirit.

He has received this gift of the Spirit by the imposition of the apostle's hands. This spirit of action, of love, and of discipline, reposed in him, bestows upon the apostolic successor all the authority and fidelity necessary for the transmission of the apostolic Gospel. But at the same time, the Holy Spirit unites him to the apostle, ever alive and operative: The Holy Spirit dwells in the apostle and in his successor ("the Holy Spirit who dwells in us"). In the mystery of the communion of saints, of the Body of Christ, the apostle and his successor, united by the Holy Spirit, continue perpetually to bring about the transmission—the tradition—of the Gospel in the Church. The apostle has the conviction that the Lord himself, uniting him to his successor, will preserve his deposit of Faith until the last day (2 Tim. 1:12). Christ, the Head of the Body, the apostolate, who sits in judgment on the faithfulness of the Church (Matt. 19:28), and the apostolic succession within the Church, which guarantees the tradition of the apostolic Gospel and transmits the Scripture and its interpretation within the Church—both of these together will watch over the true deposit of Faith.

Who—after these first apostolic successors—were to be the "men thou canst trust, men who will know how to teach it to others besides themselves" (2 Tim. 2:2), the agents of the apostolic succession, of the transmission of the Gospel?

We find in the primitive Church the continuation of this function of succession to a visitant apostleship, or one occupied with a whole region of the Church—with numerous Churches—and this in the line suggested by the letters to Timothy and Titus. St. Clement seems to have been one of these visitant apostolic successors before he became permanent at Rome; this would explain in part the responsibility he felt to the Church of Corinth in its difficulties when he addressed to it his well known letter. This letter was to be read for quite a long time in Corinth during divine services, as Dionysius testified, according to Eusebius.

St. Polycarp of Smyrna also journeyed from one Church to another, bestowing his counsel. This visitant episcopate may be explained in part by the fact that the Churches founded by St. Paul in the West probably remained for some time "presbyterian," directed by a college of presbyters, and probably presided over by members taking turns in the office of local bishop. However this may be, these "Pauline" Churches were united among themselves by apostolic successors as a visitant episcopate, which made their unity doubly sure.

St. John, having returned from Patmos to Ephesus, exercised this ministry of supervision, ordination, and foundation in that whole region of Asia Minor. The difference here was that St. John was dealing with comparatively autonomous local Churches, like that at Antioch, complete with individual local bishop, presbyterium, and deacons. St. Ignatius of Antioch is the most striking example of those early local bishops. They personified their Church, representing it while they directed it. The seven letters which open the Apocalypse testify to this episcopate, indicative of ecclesiastical organization. St. John received orders to write to the Angels of the Churches of Ephesus, Smyrna, etc. (Apoc. 2 and 3). This "Angel" (Messenger) was certainly the local bishop of the Church, who personified and represented it.

Thus, St. John the Apostle was overseer of Churches themselves provided with bishops. Then, when he died, these Churches recognized in their local bishop the apostle's successor—not as overseer or visitant, generally, but attached to a certain limited area.

In the West, the Churches were gradually to come to imitate these episcopal Churches of Asia Minor; visitant apostolic successors became attached to certain areas, and thus their episcopal office was assimiliated to that of the local presidency of the presbyterium.

As for the transmission of the Gospel in the Church, the visitant apostolic successors carried it on from one Church to another, maintaining them in unity among themselves, while relying very heavily upon the colleges of presbyters, upon local bishops, and upon ministers in charge of various functions in local Churches. When the visitant apostolic successors became attached to one place, becoming assimilated to local bishops, their ministry would become more direct. The transmission of the Gospel would be intrusted to them for the local Church. They would effect this transmission, in communion with the college of presbyters and the deacons, as chiefs of the different ministries in the Church. But they would give equal attention to the unity of the local Church with other Churches, providing for this by contacts maintained with other bishops—letters, visits, and meetings which were later to become regional synods and universal councils.

In the handing on of the Gospel, the transmission of the deposit of faith, of the already written Scriptures of the New Testament, and of the accurate interpretation of that deposit, the primitive bishop would act as the principal official in charge, but, as just indicated, in the bosom of a college of presbyters, together with the deacons, and in communion with the other bishops.[12]

This is how the circulation of apostolic letters (originally addressed to one particular Church) came about. It was gradually to enable local canons (local lists of canonical texts of the New Testament) to be combined into a single canon, accepted collectively by the bishops and their Churches. Thus the transmission of the Gospel, carried on by each bishop together with his presbyters and his deacons in his local Church, but also in communion with the other bishops of the Church, would attain the final stage of a definitive, universal canon of the New Testament.

However, even after the fixing of the canon, the tradition of the Gospel—the transmission of the Word—was to remain a living thing in the Church. The Scriptures were never to be transmitted solely as a document, but as a Word read and preached in the Church—therefore, interpreted. It has always been so; and so it is still, in every Church.

The early Church bishop, uniting in his person the ministry of an apostolic successor and the ministry of a local superintendent—that of Timothy and that of James of Jerusalem—had, then, in communion with his presbyters and his deacons, the responsibility and authority for the transmission in his Church of the apostolic deposit of faith, the Scriptures of the Old and New Testaments, the Church's common interpretation thereof, and the application of the Word of God to his own day. This common interpretation, and the proper application, he determined through his collegial relationship both with his local ministers and with the bishops of other local Churches. He also possessed the certainty of having received assistance from the Holy Spirit for the accurate transmission of the Gospel, in communion with the Church and in communion with the apostles, still active—through the apostolic writings and in the communion of saints—as envoys of Christ.

The Preface of the Apostles in the Roman liturgy emphasizes this relationship between bishops and the apostles, and this certainty of the contemporary presence of Christ's apostles in the Church for the continuation of the accurate transmission of the Gospel:

[12] G. Dix, "The Ministry in the Early Church," *The Apostolic Ministry* (London: Hodder and Stoughton, 1947), pp. 183–303.

Truly meet and just it is, reasonable and salutary, humbly to beseech thee, Lord, as Shepherd of the ages, not to desert thy flock, but through thy blessed apostles to keep it under thy continual protection, so that it may be ever led by the same heads whom thou didst choose to carry on thy work and didst place over it as its shepherds. Thus with the angels and archangels, with the thrones and dominions, and with the whole company the heavenly host, we hymn thy glory, endlessly singing: Holy, Holy, Holy, Lord God . . .

Here the liturgical text expresses very clearly the abiding quality of the apostolate—the perpetual role of the apostles in the Church. They were chosen by Christ, the eternal Shepherd, to continue his work and to govern the Church as pastors. The prayer asks the Lord to keep watch over his flock through his apostles, here and now living and present, and to set them as heads over the Churches, to lead them. The apostles are living and present here and now in the apostolic teaching of the New Testament and in the communion of saints. Bishops, considered as their successors as we are given to understand this matter in the pastoral epistles, are but the signs and instruments of this ever living and present apostolate; they have been joined to the one, single apostolic college as auxiliaries; the apostles continue to govern the Church, and transmit the Gospel, through them and by means of them. The power and authority residing in the bishops is nothing but the power and authority of the apostles operative here and now in the Church and, through their perpetual ministry, effecting the tradition of the Gospel. Their ministry, what is it but the office which Christ intrusted to them in perpetuity? And their power and authority, from whom do they hold it save from him alone, the Shepherd of the ages?

The feasts of the apostles, in the Church liturgy, serve as reminders of this government carried on by the still present and operative apostolate. Thanks to the Holy Spirit, who dwells "in us"—in the Church, in the apostles, and in the ministry which succeeds them—the heritage of the pasturage of faith can be safeguarded, and the flock led under the guidance of Christ, eternal Shepherd, and of his apostles, who are also perpetual pastors.

Within the hierarchy of the Church ministry—episcopal and presbyteral—the Holy Spirit also acts through the intermediary of men freely raised up to renew the faith and testimony of the Church. From the time of the apostles we find prophets arising to give appropriate and vital application to the Word of God in their own time and place; and we likewise find evidence of manifold gratuitously bestowed gifts of the Spirit which cause the power of Christ to shine iridescently forth. Now the point we wish to make is that all such gifts—necessary for the constant refreshment of the Church and of the Word of God—are distributed freely among Christians, and yet are harmoniously fitted into the hierarchy of the Church. The apostle, the apostolic successor, the bishop, the college of presbyters—these have the responsibility for the ministry and for unity in the Church; thus those charismatic manifestations of which we speak must make their appearance in harmony with ecclesiastical order, upon which they produce an effect of tonic invigoration.[13]

Martyrs and confessors also play their parts in the ecclesiastical hierarchy. Their fidelity is a living sermon to requicken the Church. And should the persecuted by some miracle escape martyrdom, their place in the ecclesiastical hierarchy is indicated by Hippolytus: "If a confessor has been in chains in prison for the name (of God), let not hands be imposed upon him for the office of deacon or priest, for by his profession of faith he has the dignity of the priesthood."[14]

Monks, too, offer a prophetic testimony in the Church; they shadow forth the coming Kingdom, where everything will be possessed in common, where there will be no marrying nor giving in marriage, and where all will submit in obedience to the one Shepherd. But they, too, must be subservient to the ecclesiastical hierarchy, for their prophetic testimony is without meaning save in communion with the bishops and ministers of the Church.

TRADITION, PRODUCT OF THE LIFE OF THE GOSPEL AND ITS TRANSMISSION WITHIN THE CHURCH

Thus, this existence of the Gospel in the Church and this act by which the Church transmits the Gospel produce a treasury of

[13] COLSON, pp. 354–366.

[14] *La tradition apostolique,* Sources chrétiennes 11 (Paris: Le Cerf, 1946), p. 41.

the faith which the Apostle charges his successor to *keep safe* (1 Tim. 6:20, 2 Tim. 1:14). In the pastoral epistles, this treasury appears as all the essential teaching which the Apostle had received from Christ, within the communion, intercourse, and collegiality of the other apostles. This already included certainly some brief formulas produced by the current catechesis, such as we catch echoes of in the pastoral epistles themselves (1 Tim. 2:3–7; 2 Tim. 1:8–11; Tit. 2:11–15, for example). It included also liturgical proclamations or prayers (1 Tim. 3:16; 6:15–16; 2 Tim. 2:11–13; see also Eph. 1:3–14; Phil. 2:6–11; and the eucharistic liturgy in 1 Cor. 11:23–25). And it included finally the new Scriptures which were beginning to have great authority: gospels, and the apostolic epistles (2 Tim. 3–16).

These catechetical formulas, liturgical texts, and Scriptures already made up a tangible treasury of the faith produced by both the existence and the transmission of the Gospel in the Church. The apostolic successor was exhorted to hold fast by the charge committed to him—a reference to the schooling received from the Apostle himself, who founded the authority of his own teaching and of his ministry in the Churches.

To hold fast to the trust committed to him meant holding the apostolic position in the sense that an officer holds a good tactical position in a battle. In the difficulties of the combat of faith, the apostolic successor, like a good officer of Christ and of the apostles, was to stand fast on positions gained; these would provide him with firm footing for victorious attack and for able defense.

The faithful transmission of the Gospel, and the defense of this Gospel against every distortion which would jeopardize the salvation of mankind, necessitated the safeguarding of this apostolic treasury—Christ's own Word recalled to the apostles and inspired in them by the Holy Spirit. The New Testament *Scriptures* were soon to become the preferential form of this treasury of faith: gospels written by apostles or disciples of apostles, and apostolic letters, they were to form a compilation, soon to be completed, of all the texts essential for the accurate preservation of the deposit of faith. Through these texts, read and interpreted in the liturgical assembly, the Church was able to hear—from the lips of its ministers—the very Word of God, which had been proclaimed by Christ, in the power of the Holy Spirit. The corpus of the Scriptures—the canon, or compilation of apostolic writings—was a fundamental element in the Church's life and its imparting of the Good News in the first century. Nothing could substitute for or take rank over the final authority, found here, of God's own Word. The Church was to be permanently committed to the canon of apostolic writings settled upon by the apostles' first successors.

Taking these Scriptures as fundamental, the early Church nevertheless joined to them its understanding and interpretation of the data revealed. This understanding and interpretation took shape in the Church's *liturgy,* which was to be the medium of the Gospel from generation to generation. The ancient liturgical tradition is therefore essential for the understanding of the Scriptures as the Word of God in and for the Church. It, too, comprises certain data of tradition—certainly not comparable to the authority of the apostolic Scriptures themselves, but indispensable for the authentic understanding of those Scriptures. It was the atmosphere of life and adorations where the Word of God was received and understood in obedience to Christ and in the Communion of the Holy Spirit with the apostles, ever present in the Church.

Even the catechesis—the transmission of Christian doctrine, embodying an epitome of the Gospel—was given in a liturgical framework. It was through the explanation of the mysteries, wherein the word of God was proclaimed, that the bishops, the presbyters, the Fathers imparted the truth to the catechumens and to the faithful. During the first centuries, theology was essentially liturgical; dogma was essentially doxological. The Church's worship—the mysteries—utilized the texts of Scripture, thus publicizing them and at the same time giving them a setting in tradition—the adoration and prayer of the Church—which imparted to them a living and authentic interpretation. For the catechesis, then, it was sufficient to explain the mysteries of the liturgy, where the Gospel was at once brought dramatically to life and imparted to the faithful.

The baptismal profession of faith, known under the name of the Apostles' Creed, was to spring from this liturgical catechesis as an accurate epitome of the truth contained in the apostolic writings. It was to comprise as well the fundamentals of the life and of the tradition of the Gospel, its authority deriving from its being the summary of Christ's Gospel, understood within the communion of the praying Church, under the guidance of the

Holy Spirit and of the apostolate, ever living in the communion of saints.

In accordance with Christ's institution and the apostles' faithful practice, the Church, in its liturgy, celebrated the *sacraments of baptism and the Eucharist.* If the Church safeguarded the Scriptures embraced by the catechesis of liturgy and creed in the doxological tradition, it safeguarded as well the treasury of the sacraments of the Gospel. In the liturgical mysteries of baptismal incorporation into, and eucharistic communion with, the living Christ, the Church had similar objective data of the apostolic tradition. In the sacramental life, Christ's own life was communicated to the Church along with the fulness of the Holy Spirit; and in this plenitude of life the Gospel was faithfully transmitted. In the life of the sacraments, the Church received the light of Christ and of the Spirit to enable it to understand the Word of God and to transmit it faithfully. The mysteries—or sacraments—made up part of the treasury originally given, and now transmitted, with the Gospel; they, too, were firm ground, to be held fast in the Church's victorious combat.

The apostles appointed ministers, by the *imposition of hands*—gift of the Spirit—for the preaching of the Gospel and the administration of the sacraments. Their authority as guardians of the deposit of faith, responsible for its accurate transmission, they passed on to "men thou canst trust," apostolic successors and guardians of the Church. This imposition of hands—conducted in obedience to the Holy Spirit, with due discrimination and with regard for ecclesiastical order—was designed to provide the Church continuously with ministers (manifestations of the ministry of Christ), and was also among the objective data of the apostolic tradition.

By this ordination, the Holy Spirit was given to men who became instruments of Christ in his building up of his Church into a priestly kingdom, a royal race of priests, a corps of prophets in the midst of the world. These instruments, these ordained ministers, put their lives at Christ's disposition—lent him their minds, their hearts, their lips, their actions, so that thereby Christ—Apostle, Prophet, and Teacher—might proclaim his Word, and so that, as Priest and Intercessor, he might administer the sacraments, give praise, and make intercession, and also so that, as

King, Bishop, and Shepherd, he might lead his people—his flock—in unity and obedience into the Kingdom. The imposition of hands made up another part of the apostolic trust to be safeguarded, for the laying on of hands engendered ever anew these necessary signs and instruments of the episcopate, pastorate, and diaconate of Jesus Christ in his Church, so that the Church might become a prophetic and priestly kingdom whereby God might be glorified, and whereby the world might believe.[15]

This ordination of minsters of the Church was an apostolic institution and a necessary part of the treasury to be guarded because it produced for the Church the signs and instruments of Christ's ministry through the Word and the sacraments. Without this ordination, the Church could not have been assured that the ministers it appointed to their various offices, by reason of their vocation and their training, were really invested with the power of the Holy Spirit for their ministry, were really fitted for transmitting the Word of God and administering the sacraments of Christ in the truth of the Spirit, and were really authentic agents of the transmission of the Gospel in the Church.

True enough, God is free; and the Spirit breathes where he will. Christ proclaims his word and manifests his presence through this prophet, that witness, or some other member of the faithful; in fact, where two or three are gathered together in his name, there is he in the midst of them. In all this he is by no means restricted to ordained ministers. But ordination was indispensable for transmitting the Holy Spirit as uniting the apostles with their successors and their collaborators in faithful guardianship of the deposit of faith.

This imposition of hands may have been given by a college of presbyters—created by an apostle—acting as a collective bishop: "A special grace has been given to thee; prophecy awarded it, and the imposition of the presbyters' hands went with it; do not let it suffer from neglect" (1 Tim. 4:14). It may have been given by the apostle himself: "I would remind thee to fan the flame of that special grace which God kindled in thee, when my hands were laid upon thee" (2 Tim. 1:6). It might be given by the apostolic

[15] H. J. Wotherspoon and J. M. Kirkpatrick, *A Manual of Church Doctrine According to the Church of Scotland*, London: Oxford University Press, 1960.

successor: "As for the imposition of hands, do not bestow it inconsiderately" (1 Tim. 5:22). But in any case it was still the collegiate apostolate which, in the name of Christ, joined to itself successors or collaborators by an imposition of hands conferring the Holy Spirit "of action, of life, and of discipline" for the accurate transmission of the Gospel within the Church through the Word of God and the sacraments of his presence. The Holy Spirit was granted through the imposition of the apostles' hands (Acts 8:18). The apostles—as we have so often repeated in these pages—are ever present in the Church; and it is they who continue to insure the uninterrupted succession of the ministry for the faithful safeguarding of the deposit of faith and for the authentic transmission of the Gospel.

This is what the Church later intended to signify when it assigned the administration of ordination to bishops exclusively, since they are signs of the presence of the apostles in the Church for its goverance. Yet the conception of a collective episcopate consisting of a college of presbyters for the administration of ordination was not alien or contrary to the practice of the early Church, in certain regions. The important thing was that the bishop—whether single or collective—have the intention of acting with the apostles—in communion with them, and as an agent in the apostolic succession—with the intention of conferring the gift of the Holy Spirit upon new ministers, for the purpose of making them signs and instruments of the episcopate, the pastorate, or the diaconate of Jesus Christ in his Body, the Church. The minister of ordination was the apostle, always present in the Church, through the intermediary of his successor, the bishop, whether individual or collegiate. Most commonly, combining the two traditions, the Church gave recognition to—as the minister of ordination—the bishop, apostolic successor, acting in and with the college of presbyters, apostolic collaborators.[16]

The ordination of a pastor is the act whereby a Christian is signed with the character of shepherd; it is *a prayer* to the Holy Spirit, who confers the gifts necessary for the ministry; it is a *stamp of genuinity:* the imposition of hands is the sign that these

[16] J. M. Barcklay, "La signification de l'ordination," *Verbum Caro,* XLIII (1957), 226–250; T. F. Torrance, *Conflict and Agreement in the Church,* Vol. II, London: Lutterworth, 1960.

gifts of the Spirit are actually bestowed in accordance with the specific petition expressed by the Church; it is a *dedication,* an offering of a new servant to God; it is a *begetting,* a transmission of life and vigor—the vitality and power of the Spirit, given by existent ministers to new ministers from generation to generation: thus, only pastors can take part in the imposition of hands upon new pastors.[17]

The ordination of a deacon is the act whereby a Christian is stamped with the character of assistant in the pastoral ministry: it, too, is a prayer, an attestation of genuinity, a dedication, and a begetting, in accordance with the specific intention of consecrating a deacon, assistant in the pastoral ministry.[18]

The consecration of a bishop is the act whereby a pastor is *designated* as head of a local or regional Church and *blessed* for the exercise of this charge; the consecration of a bishop, too, is a prayer, an attestation of genuinity, a dedication, and a begetting; a bishop does not receive a *new* pastoral ministry: his pastoral office is given a broader territorial extension and a greater ecumenical responsibility; the bishop becomes a pastor of pastors, and a sign of the unity of each Church with the others: that is why he is consecrated by other bishops, and why he presides at ordinations of new ministers.

But—while pastors and deacons are made collaborators in the apostolate (which is one and the same for the whole Church)—the bishop is made an apostolic successor, in the sense that he is the sign of the apostles' presence and government, and that he insures, with them and with the other ministers, the faithful transmission of the Gospel, and the safeguarding and intact delivery of the charge committed to the apostles—the deposit of faith.

In Churches of presbyterian organization, it is important to emphasize the episcopal character of the college of ordained pastors acting collectively in the government of the Church in the transmission of the gospel and in the ordination of new ministers, normally under the presidency of a superintendent (moderator or regional president). This presbyteral government, too, must sig-

[17] J.-J. von Allmen, "La vie pastorale," *Verbum Caro,* XL (1956), 187–189.

[18] J. Colson, *La fonction diaconale aux origines de l'Eglise,* Paris: Desclée de Brouwer, 1960.

nify the government of that single apostolate, instituted and sent forth by Christ. Everything, that is, in this matter, must exhibit the ministry of Christ through his apostles in and for the Church. It is not possible, for example, for laymen to take part in the imposition of hands upon new ministers, for their doing so would signify that the ministry is a delegation from the people of God, instead of a gift from above, coming down from Christ and the Holy Spirit.[19]

The rediscovery, by Churches of presbyterian structure, of the ministry of the bishop surrounded by his college of pastors, would be the surest way to make clear the present-day role of the one and only apostolate in the Church, and to avoid any interpretation of the ministry as a species of democratic delegation. This rediscovery—wholly within the legitimate line of the Reform—would have a capital ecumenical bearing.

The Word of God—contained in the Scriptures, embraced and vitalized by the Church's liturgy, transmitted by ordained ministers, under the guardianship and conduct of the apostles and their successors—may happen to be challenged. In that case, a difficulty arises in the Church, for it may then be called upon to make an official decision, defining the truth in the matter and outlawing the error involved, in accordance with its pastoral responsibility.

The Church, therefore, may proceed to convoke a *council*—regional or ecumenical, depending on the importance and extent of the controversy. In doing so, it is following the example of the apostles and of the presbyters of Jerusalem who met to look into the question that had come up, namely, whether converts from paganism were required to conform to the Mosaic Law (Acts 15:5–29). Peter, the first among the apostles, and James, supervisor of the presbyters of Jerusalem, presented their point of view. Then the experiences of the apostles Barnabas and Paul were heard; and the discussion terminated with the decision to send to Antioch a delegation armed with a letter settling the question in a moderate way.

It was the apostles and presbyters, with the agreement of the whole Church, who decided upon this mission (Acts 15:22). The apostles, as responsible for the accurate transmission of the

[19] Wotherspoon and Kirkpatrick, pp. 93–98.

Gospel, and the presbyters, their local collaborators, conveyed in their decision the agreement of the whole Church of Jerusalem, considered as the Mother Church. The best-established Greek text speaks of a meeting of the apostles and the presbyters solely (not of the Church: Acts 15:6), yet the mention of these only does not rule out the presence of other Christians of Jerusalem, with the Judaizers, whose case was on trial. However this may be, the emphasis in the account is placed upon the part played by the apostles and the presbyters, and upon the speeches of the apostles Peter, Paul, and Barnabas, and upon the supervisor James. During the speeches, the whole company, it is reported (Acts 15:12), kept silence. The Judaizers, the converted Pharisees, were silent, and probably allowed themselves to be persuaded by Peter, the first apostle, by Paul and Barnabas, but above all by James, supervisor of Jerusalem, who, with considerable authority, proposed a diplomatic form of settlement (Acts 15:19–21). It was the apostles and presbyters whose decision it was to send a delegation to Antioch, but the whole Church of Jerusalem—the Mother Church, directly affected by the problem—was in agreement with them.

The apostles and the presbyters embraced in their council the communion of the entire Church, which was to reach its agreement in their normative decision. This decision was not the act of the apostles alone—Peter, John, Paul—whose ministry extended to the universal Church—but also of the local presbyters, and above all of their supervisor, the apostolic auxiliary, James, head of the Mother Church at Jerusalem, whose authority and opinion were recognized as the wisdom of God.

The apostles and presbyters could say with confidence, in their letter to Antioch, "The Holy Spirit and we have decided to impose upon you no obligations save those that cannot be spared you . . . " (Acts 15:28). In this capital conciliar decision, which had to be the thing which would re-establish unity and give proper direction to the Church's career, the apostles and presbyters acted with the certitude that the Holy Spirit decided with them: that he and the Church, whole and entire, were one; that he expressed himself through them, the apostles and presbyters of the Mother Church.

When the unity of the Church hinged thus upon a capital question, the Holy Spirit intervened to insure the accurate transmission of the Gospel by the apostles and their auxiliaries. The Holy Spirit spoke here by the mouth of the whole Church, through Peter, Paul, Barnabas, and the other universal apostles, and through the presbyters and overseer of Jerusalem. Collegially, the apostles, the auxiliary apostles, and the local ministers expressed the will of the Holy Spirit for the whole Church and in communion with it.[20] They accomplished an act of faithful transmission of the Gospel, and this act produced a normative document, the letter to the Church at Antioch. This letter was dispatched by the intermediary not only of Paul and Barnabas, whose known—and wholly justified—convictions in favor of the converts from paganism might tend to diminish the authority of the document from Jerusalem, but also of Judas Barsabas and Silas, leading men at Jerusalem, charged with transmitting the message orally as well. Thus, the written document was accompanied by live transmission. The Church did not make texts and laws its sole instruments; the faithful transmission of the Gospel was accomplished through the word of men commissioned by the apostles of Christ, proclaiming the very Word of God contained in the apostolic writings.

The Council of Jerusalem left to posterity a document, an evidence of the faithful transmission of the Gospel under the management of the apostles and of their auxiliaries, and an expression of an authentic interpretation of the deposit of faith.

At other difficult moments in its history, the Church, in response to its pastoral responsibility, was to judge it necessary to convoke still other councils. These were to consist of the gathering together of all the bishops and representatives of local Churches in a universal college, united to the apostles, who were to continue governing the Church in the name of Christ. Through these councils, the Holy Spirit was to continue to insure the accurate transmission of the Gospel—the authentic tradition of the teaching of the apostles—precisely at such times as dispute or division would threaten to set the Church off on a wrong path were it not assured, precisely, of this assistance on the part of the Holy Spirit, who guards the apostolic deposit of faith in the agreement of the

[20] B. Botte, "La Collégialité dans le Nouveau Testament et chez les Pères apostoliques," *Le concile et les conciles* (Paris: Cerf-Chevetogne, 1960), pp. 1–18.

apostolic successors and their auxiliaries, expressing in turn the agreement of the whole Church.

Thus the decisions reached and the documents produced by these councils, to which we look back in history, furnish certain data—a normative interpretation—of the apostolic deposit of faith. Of course, these conciliar dogmas are no substitute for the Gospel, but they are the authentic understanding of the Gospel as that understanding is found in a trustworthy tradition. Now this understanding may not have been immediately explicit and complete; it is on these grounds that a subsequent council may add to the decisions of a preceding one, clarifying them, making them more explicit, filling them out. The Church's tradition, we repeat, remains a living one; it does not work by producing mosaics of conciliar definitions, nor is it itself a manual of definitions; it is the living transmission of God's Word in every age, fitted to the particular needs and difficulties of each. Given the part played by the Holy Spirit in a council ("The Holy Spirit and we have decided . . ." Acts 15:28), the dogmas proclaimed therein are an authentic expression of the faithful tradition of the apostolic deposit of faith. They cannot be denied or contradicted; they can only be rendered still more explicit or full by a new conciliar intervention on the part of the Holy Spirit.

Thus—to sum up—the Church's tradition, viewed as the fundamental objective elements exhibiting the faithful guardianship of the apostolic treasury of faith, comprises the following:

The Scriptures of the New Testament, the revealed data of the Gospel of salvation, written form of the apostolic memoirs and reflections, these being inspired by the Holy Spirit in accordance with Christ's promise.

The sacraments of baptism and the Eucharist, revealed institutions of Christ, insuring God's redemptive presence and operation in his Church.

The imposition of hands, revealed institution of the apostles, insuring the gift of the Holy Spirit for the accurate transmission of the deposit of faith by the proclamation of God's Word and the administration of the just-named sacraments of his redemptive presence and operation.

The liturgy, institution of the Church praying before the Father, through Christ, in the Holy Spirit, in which the Word of God is read, preached, and understood, the sacraments administered, and the mysteries of salvation lived, and in which God, one and threefold, is adored, praised, and petitioned.

The creeds—that called the Apostles' and that of Nicaea and Constantinople, institutions of the Church professing its faith, ecumenical summaries of the faith in accordance with the faithful tradition of the Gospel by the Holy Spirit in the Church.

The dogmas of the first seven truly ecumenical councils, institutions of the teaching Church met together through its representatives under the direction of the Holy Spirit, in communion with the apostles, to discharge its pastoral responsibility by proclaiming the truth and casting out error, and by thus insuring the accurate transmission of the authentic Gospel, of the apostolic treasury of faith.

We have seen that the Scriptures—revelation of the Gospel to the Church—and tradition—transmission of the Gospel in the Church—were strictly connected. Now we must seek to understand how the Scriptures were understood by and in the Church with an eye to the faithful transmission of the apostolic treasury of faith. In the next score of pages, which bring this section on "Tradition" to a virtual close, we shall see that the understanding of the Scriptures given by the Church may be described as catholic, doxological, and missionary.

TRADITION, CATHOLIC UNDERSTANDING OF SCRIPTURE

In the two ecumenical creeds the Church is called catholic. To be correctly understood, this description must be seen in relationship with its biblical source.

St. Paul wrote that God, the Father to whom glory belongs, has put everything under Christ's dominion, "and made him the head to which the whole Church is joined, so that the Church is his body, the completion of him who everywhere and in all things is complete" (Eph. 1:22–23).

The Church is catholic because it is the Body of Christ, the fulness of him who is Fulness itself. "Catholic" expresses a quality of totality and fulness. The Church, then, is Catholic from four fundamental points of view:

First, the Church is catholic because it both bears within itself and transmits the totality and the fulness of the truth—in the Word and in the sacraments. Christ himself publishes the Gospel through the Scriptures and through the preaching of the ministers of the Church; he is present and operative through the sacraments. No fulness greater than that is to be found outside the Church. And such totality and fulness render the Church catholic. Certainly the human beings—sinful men—who make up the Church may fail to discern this fulness of truth, or may obscure it; yet it does not thereby cease to exist; it exists in the Word of God and in the sacraments of his presence despite sin and error on the part of individual members.

Secondly, the Church is catholic because it both bears within itself and transmits the totality and fulness of life, and because conversely it envelops and integrates into the Body of Christ the totality of human existence—of each human member. The whole life of man is incorporated into Christ's life in his Church. Nothing about a Christian can remain outside this full and total life of the Church. It embraces and engages him totally. In its liturgy and in its moral instruction, in its service and in its mission, the Church penetrates to the entirety of a man's being, marks it, and makes it captive to obedience to Christ; for the Church concerns itself not alone with souls; it forms man in the totality of his life—spiritual and intellectual, mental and physical. That is why the liturgy—God's people engaged in prayer—is an activity which includes words, actions, and symbols. And that is why the Church's moral teaching is of import for every area of life—emotional and sexual, as well as religious or social.

This catholic fulness of truth and life define the Church also as holy—holy by virtue of the holy things which it contains within itself (the sacraments and the truth), and holy by virtue of the sanctified beings which live in it on the life of Christ. Here, the designations holy and catholic overlap.

Thirdly, the Church is catholic because it is rich in the totality and fulness of its history. It lives in the continuity of time, which is ever enriching its experience. In the course of the centuries, because it has been forced (under the providence of God) to deal with history, its understanding of Revelation has been deepened and diversified. In its life, from generation to generation, it has been united to the apostles and by the communion of saints. All who in the course of history have contributed to the Church's progress in time are alive today in Christ, with the Father in unity with the Holy Spirit, and endow the Church with all the richness of their experience and their sanctity. This sense of tradition, of continuity, of the Church's unity in time in the union of saints triumphant, makes a living thing of its apostolicity, its connection without discontinuity to the apostolate of the Twelve instituted by Christ. The Church is rich with an apostolic fulness ever present during the course of the centuries. Here, the terms apostolic and catholic overlap.

Fourthly, the Church is catholic because it is rich with the totality and fulness of creation. Spread throughout the entire world, it embraces all nations, all races, and all cultures, and would unite them in all their diversity. Not divided but enriched by what each contributes, the Church tends towards visible unity over the face of the globe. The structural universality of the Church militant manifests its visible spatial unity amid the richness and diversity of the variety of human contributions, signs of its catholicity and commensurate with the totality and plenitude of creation which it embraces. Here, the terms one and catholic overlap.[21]

The catholicity of the Church, then, as fulness of Christ's truth contained in it, is the very object of our study of the faithful tradition of the apostolic Gospel. As for the catholicity of the Church as the fulness of Christ's life in it, this we shall touch upon more particularly in the following two sections on the doxological and missionary understanding of the Scriptures. We shall devote a number of pages at this point only to envisaging the problem of tradition as the understanding of Scripture achieved by the Church

[21] G. Bardy, *La Théologie de l'Eglise de saint Clément de Rome à saint Irénée . . . de saint Irénée au concile de Nicée,* Paris: Le Cerf, 1945, 1947 (*Unam Sanctam,* XIII, XIV); H. de Lubac, *Méditation sur l'Eglise,* Paris: Aubier, 1953 (*Théologie* XXVII); W. A. Visser 't Hooft, *Le renouveau de l'Eglise* (Nouvelle série théologique 1), Geneva: Labor et Fides, 1956; *The Pressure of Our Common Calling,* London: SCM, 1959.

as catholic in time and space. This catholic understanding of the Scriptures is an understanding in accord with the *nature of the Church,* which is the fulness of Him who possesses all fulness.

1) *Catholicity in time*

The apostolate of the Twelve appointed by Christ joined the Church to Israel and cemented the unity of the two Covenants: the twelve patriarchs of the twelve tribes had their successors in the twelve apostles. This apostolate also insured the continuity of the Church in time: from the Pentecost of the Holy Spirit until the return of Christ, the apostles lead and govern the Church by their doctrine and their power, faithfully transmitted in the ministry of the Church. On the Last Day, the Church's fidelity will be judged by Christ and the apostles. The apostolate is therefore always present in the communion of saints, with the multitude of the faithful and of the ministers of the Church. Through the course of history, these have undertaken to transmit the apostolic teaching, the authentic Gospel. The Church, therefore, grasps its fidelity to Christ's apostles in the measure that it is conscious of its historical continuity and discerns their voice in the whole of its tradition.

In fact, what the apostles uttered under the inspiration of the Holy Spirit and what is found in the Scriptures is constantly more profoundly grasped in the confrontation by the Church's ministry —under God's providence—of the conditions of history. The apostles are always present therein, in the communion of saints, to apply their changeless doctrine to the conditions of the times and to govern the Church in its transmission of the Gospel to the world. To be attentive to all these applications of the Gospel to the various forces of history is to understand the richness and diversity of the unique Gospel. In this treasure-house of manifold explanations and applications of the truth, the Church will find the secret of a new explanation and a new application of the ageless Gospel to our own age. It will recognize in the immense work of the saints of all ages the essential work of the apostles, ever living in it and governing it, ever insuring the faithful tradition of the apostolic teaching—of the Gospel of Christ.

The work of the Church's Fathers and of its great Doctors will bring it an understanding of the richness of truth; the development of the liturgy will enable it to penetrate the depths of the mystery of piety; the courage, the imagination, and the sacrifices of so many missionaries, monks, martyrs, ministers, and layfolk will give it some appreciation of the measure of the power of the charity of Christ.

It is most particularly at crucial moments in its history, when menace to its unity leads it to convoke a council, that the Church enjoys this presence of the Holy Spirit and the apostles as it confronts the world and its powers. It has the assurance that the gates of hell will not prevail against it, and as at the first council in Jerusalem (Acts 15:28), that the Holy Spirit, the apostles, and the "trustworthy men" of whom Paul wrote to Timothy, ministers of unity, one in the Body of Christ, will be able to determine which way the road of truth lies, and which way error.

With the Roman Catholic Church, the Orthodox Church recognizes the dogmatic authority of the first seven ecumenical councils, but holds councils after the seventh century to be partial, Western councils.[22] In the sixteenth century, the Reform recognized the authority of the first four councils, at any rate, as faithful expression of the Scriptures. Calvin wrote:

> Thereupon we are glad to accept such early councils as those of Nicaea, Constantinople, the first at Ephesus, Chalcedon, and the like, held in order to condemn the errors and wicked opinions of heretics; we bear them, I say, honor and reverence, for the articles that were defined there. These councils, that is, contain naught but a pure and natural interpretation of the Scriptures, which the holy Fathers through a good use of prudence so used as to overthrow the enemies of Christianity.[23]

The various professions of faith repeat the affirmations and condemnations of these councils.[24] The fifth and sixth councils echo the third and fourth; the seventh, dealing with images, was less gratifying to the Reformers, who were struggling against certain superstitions. Yet it is plain enough that if one accepts the

[22] P. Evdokimov, *L'orthodoxie* (Neuchâtel and Paris: Delachaux et Niestlé, 1959), pp. 159–161; J. Meyendorff, *L'Eglise orthodoxe hier et aujourd'hui* (Paris: Le Seuil, 1960), pp. 35–40.

[23] *Institution chrétienne,* 1560, IV, IX, 8 (Geneva: Labor et Fides, IV, 163).

[24] For example, the Rochelle Confession, Articles V and VI.

first four councils on account of their ecumenicity, then one must also accept the three that followed them and had, after all, the same ecumenicity. The first seven councils vigorously asserted the apostolic teaching concerning the Trinity and Christ: God in himself, and in the incarnation.[25]

The first Council of Nicaea (325) discussed the claims of Arius, priest of Alexandria, who denied that Christ had a divinity equal to the Father's. He denied the real divinity of the person of the Son, consubstantial with the Father.

The first Council of Constantinople (381) definied the divinity of the Holy Spirit against the claims of Macedonius, patriarch of Constantinople.

Thus, in the fourth century, the first two ecumenical councils gave precise formulation to the dogma of the Trinity, epitomized in the Creed of Nicaea and Constantinople. This dogma is not explicitly in the Scriptures, but it is plain enough that God, being one, reveals himself there in three distinct persons: the Father, the Son, and the Holy Spirit. Contemplation of the three divine persons, revealed in the Scriptures, was the ground upon which the dogma of the Trinity became defined in the faith of the Church. But the opposition of Arius, proposing the difficulty that three equal persons in God was a concept repugnant to monotheism, led the Church to define its faith still more precisely.

No, it was not philosophical speculation on the unity of the divine nature diversified in three personalities as modes of the existence of God that led the Church to the dogma of the Trinity. It was pondering the sacred texts, on the one hand, and then the rationalist objection of Arius, on the other. This led it to discover that, in Revelation, God exists and manifests himself in three distinct persons and yet that he is but one God. In the history of salvation, God manifests his being in the three distinct persons of the Trinity and yet there is never any question of several gods, but only of one God. Basing its thought on the biblical contemplation of the three divine persons and the biblical affirmation

[25] CALVIN, after the text cited above, continues: "Similarly, in some of the interpretations of the councils held thereafter, we detect a fine zeal and evident signs of learning, prudence, and intelligence; but the way of the world is from bad to worse, and it is easy to see how little by little the Church fell from its due purity," *ibid.*, IV, IX, 8, p. 163.

of the singleness of God, the Church was assisted by the Holy Spirit and the apostles in publishing the truth of Christ's Gospel on the subject of the Trinity and Unity of God, in these first two ecumenical councils.

The Council of Ephesus (431) intended to do nothing but repeat and give a more precise formulation of the Christological faith of the Council of Nicaea: "The holy Synod defined that it is unlawful for anyone to profess, write, or compose any other profession of faith but that defined by the holy Fathers assembled at Nicaea with the Holy Spirit. . . ." In a way, there has been but one council—that of Nicaea—repeated in different ways by the subsequent ones. For if the Virgin Mary was "called mother of God *(theotokos, deipara)*" by the Fathers of the Council, it is because they wished to proclaim without ambiguity that Jesus had been really God incarnate from the first instant of his existence as a man—from his conception. Thus it is not possible to distinguish—after the manner of Nestorius, condemned at the Council—a human person and a divine person in Christ in such a way as to be able to speak of the existence of the one and the existence of the other separately. In giving birth to the man Jesus, Mary became mother of God in his birth here on earth.

In condemning Pelagianism, the Council affirmed also the full substitution of Christ for our humanity in the work of salvation. Just as Christ had been God incarnate in a man from the moment of his conception, he had descended to the depths of our human misery. He had not come as meeting our efforts half way, but took our human place to accomplish from the lowest reach of our human condition the total work of our salvation.

The Council of Chalcedon (451) stabilized the definitions of the Council of Ephesus in rebuffing the monophysite interpretation being given the latter. Chalcedon defined that recognizing in Christ only one, divine person did not mean that one must confuse in him divinity and humanity, and to the point of seeing the latter absorbed by the former. Jesus Christ is true God and true Man, two natures in one person, without confusion or division.

The second Council of Constantinople (553) reaffirmed the position of the Council of Ephesus, rebuffing Nestorian ideas which reappeared after Chalcedon and affirming the unity of the person of Jesus Christ.

The third Council of Constantinople (680) reaffirmed the position of the Council of Chalcedon is rejecting the tenets of monothelitism, according to which there was only one will in Christ. It defined that, conformably with the Chalcedonian dogma of the two natures, there had been two wills and two activities in Christ, without either of these two being contrary. Christ had two wills, without division between them but without confusion.

One can notice the same balancing and the same re-established equilibrium, like that of a pendulum, between the Councils of Ephesus and Chalcedon and the second and third of Constantinople. All four repeated and expressed more precisely the teaching of the first councils of Nicaea and of Constantinople, epitomized in the Creed. Just as trinitary equilibrium was established in the affirmation of the unicity and trinity of God, so the Christological equilibrium was established in the affirmation of the unity of person and the duality of natures, wills, and operations in Christ.

Thus there is a real continuity and unity among the first six ecumenical councils. They all affirm the same truth about Christ-God, second person of the Trinity, incarnate as a real man, for the salvation of lost humanity.

This same continuity and unity is still found in the seventh ecumenical council, the second Council of Nicaea (787), which—against the iconoclasts—declared lawful the respect given images in the liturgy. The presence of images of Christ and the saints in the liturgy and the respect given them are a sign of the catholicity of redemption. Christ God was incarnate in such a way, and his redemption so penetrated the depths of the creature, that artistic representation—using colors and forms (symbol of the consecration of the whole of creation to the Creator)—is capable of being touched by the power of the Gospel and is able to transmit the Gospel in the manner natural to itself. In a way, an image used in the liturgy is the sign of the universal redemption, which reaches the whole of creation and enables the whole of created nature to be offered by the Church in praise of the Creator. Images of Christ and of the saints, intended by the artist and by the Church for the glory of the Creator, become the symbol of a true adoration, and because of the incarnation's work of restoring the whole of creation, a foreshadowing of the Kingdom of God. The Council said: "The respect given an icon passes to the person who is the subject of it; one who venerates an icon venerates in it the substance of what it represents." Here we find affirmed in its ultimate consequences the power of the redemption due to the incarnation of God as man, which penetrated creation whole and entire and rendered it worthy to glorify—and to invite man to glorify—the Creator. The lawfulness of images in the liturgy is a consequence of Christology, for it makes clear that the incarnation has the power to re-establish the whole of creation to its liturgical function of adoration of the Creator. It is in this sense that the second Council of Nicaea is the legitimate outgrowth of the first six ecumenical councils and remains in full unity and continuity with them.

The ecumenicity of the first seven councils results from the fact that they treated of fundamental problems confronting the whole Church, and that the whole Church was represented in them. We have already directed attention to their unity and continuity and to the fact that together they formed but one great dogmatic definition concerning the Trinity, Christ, the incarnation, and the redemption. They all stemmed from the first Council—and the Creed—of Nicaea.[26]

Other councils were held in the West, treating of capital problems, but of interest chiefly to the Western Churches—the East, after the schism, being out of the picture here. Of course, the second Council of Lyons (1274) and the Council of Florence (1438) attempted a union between the two, but the entente was of short duration.

The real ecumenicity of a future council will require the presence of all Christians now separated and desirous of regaining their visible unity. The Second Vatican Council, the Panorthodox Synod, the World Council at Geneva—these are steps towards the new ecumenical council of the future. When it appears, then, in a real desire for unity, all the Churches together can take up the major Roman Catholic, Orthodox, and Protestant affirmations, to discover together the fulfilment and the explicit form of what they have been formulating individually.

In fact, the ecumenicity of a council derives to it from the

[26] On the importance and the primacy of the Council of Nicaea and the first four councils, see Y. Congar, "La primauté des quatre premiers conciles oecuméniques, origine, destin, sens et portée d'un thème traditionnel," *Le concile et les conciles* (Paris: Le Cerf-Chevetogne, 1960), pp. 75 ff.

actual or potential participation of authorized representatives of all baptized persons, firmly resolved to make every effort to maintain or recover, together, their visible unity.[27]

We have seen how the accurate transmission of the Gospel was carried on through the ecumenical councils of the undivided Church. This transmission was achieved ordinarily by the authorized ministry of the Church, which proclaimed the Gospel and administered the sacraments of Christ's presence and activity. Ordinarily; but when a problem arose, or a division of opinion, or a heresy, the universal Church met in council "with the Holy Spirit" (in the words of the Council of Ephesus), with the certainty that the Holy Spirit and the apostles would assure it of their assistance—just as at Jerusalem—to show it the way and to lead it to a true understanding of Revelation, of the Sacred Scriptures.

It was not a question of discovering some new truth on each of these occasions, but simply of understanding afresh and more profoundly the single mystery of Christ. There was not, then, a dogmatic development from council to council in the sense that time brought truth gradually to ripen. The truth, given once and

[27] We may ask why the dogma of papal infallibility, promulgated in 1870, at the first Vatican Council, which called forcefully into question the conciliar positions taken at the Council of Constance (1414–1418), might not be legitimately called into question, in its turn, in a future truly ecumenical council; why what the bishops of the infallibilist majority at the first Vatican Council were allowed, in relationship to the bishops of the Council of Constance, might not be permitted to the Fathers of a future council, in relationship to definitions which were incomplete because conceived in the divided state of present-day Christianity. See the excellent article of R. AUBERT, "L'ecclésiologie au concile du Vatican," *Le concile et les conciles* (Paris: Le Cerf-Chevetogne, 1960), pp. 245–284. J. DE TORQUEMADA, defender of papal primacy at the Council of Basle, however, declared of the pope: *"quamdiu catholicus est, verus summus pontifex est*—as long as he is Catholic, he is the true sovereign pontiff" (*Oratio syn.*, p. 71); and again, "Should it happen that all the Fathers, met in a general council, were in agreement on a definition of faith, and the pope alone opposed to it, I should say that in my opinion we should have to follow the opinion of the council, and not that of the pope . . . in that case, the council is superior to the pope, not in jurisdictional power, but by superiority of discriminatory judgment and extent of information" (*Oratio syn.*, p. 58); and there is no doubt that Pope Eugene IV accepted this position, at the time of the Council of Basle.

for all, did not—does not—change. But prompted by deviations from the faith, the councils, in the course of the centuries, contrived contemporaneous expressions of that one and fully matured truth—expressions adapted to repelling error and to insuring accurate transmission of the Gospel.

The resultant series of conciliar expressions of the unchanging truth also progressively revealed more and more of its diversity and richness, enabling the Church to penetrate it ever more profoundly. That is why, in the first seven councils, we can remark such striking unity and continuity. After the first Council of Nicaea had given precise formulation to the dogma of the Trinity and of the divinity of Christ, the subsequent six councils had only to take up again these fundamental truths, look further into them, give them fresh expression, present them in modern guise. We have noted how much each council quoted those preceding it, and especially that of Nicaea. Each time that the Church convoked a council it was aiming to do nothing else than to return to the fundamental truths of scriptural faith expressed at Nicaea, to draw from them all their consequences, and thus to give accurate transmission to the apostolic Gospel by steering clear of error.

Thus the Church expressed its identity throughout the passage of time, its fidelity to the apostolic Gospel, and its submission to the Holy Spirit, who by the deathless ministry of the apostles safeguards the Body of Christ in its integrity.

The further the Church progresses in history the more it is confronted by events, ideas, developments, indeed whole civilizations, which oblige it to search the Christian mystery to discover its further riches and its possibilities for presentation suitable to the new circumstances. Thus the Church discovers and expresses the catholic breadth of the apostolic truth, and its ability to answer the needs and problems of every age. Tradition—a series of different expressions of one and the same truth—constitutes the catholicity of the Church in time; it displays the manifold facets of the fulness of truth contained in the Sacred Scriptures.

2) *Catholicity in space*

Tradition—the faithful transmission of the Gospel—includes the participation of humanity in all its diversity. If differences in time lead the Church to an ever more rich expression of the changeless truth, differences in place and among races and cultures in the whole extent of the created world, play an identical part. The wholest and truest understanding of Revelation involves not only a reference to the history of the Church and particularly to the ecumenical councils, but also an introduction to the various forms the Church shows all over the face of the globe today.

Today the Church meets more than ever before the infinite diversity of the world; and this diversity affects its understanding of the truth. The diversity of creation as intended by God, in contact with the undifferentiated truth, simply seizes it in all its richness. The Holy Spirit, poured out upon all creation, leads the mind of each individual in accordance with the latter's own temperament to an understanding of Revelation. And this various understanding of the unvaried truth has shadings according with the various human characters formed in the school of different cultures.

It would be an insult to creation, and hence to the Creator, to consider this human diversity as a handicap which must be removed through an enforced uniformity of minds. The faithful transmission of the Gospel involves the collaboration of the Church, whole and entire, spread over the whole earth. Instead of imposing any one particular culture as the proper one to give expression to the truth, the Church must be on the alert for all the echoes which the Gospel produces in every corner of the world. Too long has European culture, Latin culture, pressed to impose itself upon the entire world as the only culture adequate for the expression of the Gospel truth. Today the awakening of Asia and of Africa has enforced a degree of modesty upon European culture in the Church. Tradition today must spring from contact between East and West, and between Europe and Africa. The "young Churches," newly autonomous, are due to play a decisive part in the present-day tradition of the Gospel. Taking over the burden from Christianity's tired, old cultures, it is they perhaps who will insure the faithful transmission of the Gospel to future generations.

Here, in fact, the Church is called upon for some adaptability and youthfulness. A reactionary or conservative attitude is an impossible one for the Church, believing as it does in the operation of the Holy Spirit, acting constantly through the apostles to expand the Gospel into contemporary life. Just how is this present-day application to be brought about if the Church remains hidebound in outdated cultures? There is no question, naturally, of giving up the biblical form of Revelation; for the fact of the incarnation of God in one certain place and time has given a dateless value and efficaciousness to the conceptions of the mystery of God utilized by the Sacred Scriptures. Yet, while employing biblical concepts in its grasp of the unchanging truth, the Church is confronted with the present-day world in all its diversity, and must express this changeless truth in the manifold languages of the places, races, and cultures which its duty is to unite to the tradition of the Gospel.

This diversity of creation in space contributes to an ever richer undertsanding of Revelation. In making room for the world's diversity, tradition manifests the Church's catholicity in space. Approached and understood in the light of this spatial catholicity of tradition, the unchanging truth manifests its plenitude wherein each individual, of whatever provenance, is able to make the Gospel of Christ a true penetration of his own particular humanity.

The presence of this variety of cultures in the tradition of the Gospel is very important in enabling the Church to distinguish what is essential truth and what is only accidental expression of that truth. It is certain, for instance, that various conceptions of the universe in the course of history have affected the development of theological expressions of the Christian mystery. From the Judaic cosmology to the Ptolemaic, from this to the Copernican or Newtonian, from the Newtonian to that of Einstein, it is clear that there has been a succession of revolutions in the theological expression of the immutable truth.

The resurrection and ascension of Christ, historical facts and truths of the faith, cannot be conceived in the same way by a man of our day as by a contemporary of Christ. The biblical images of "down here on earth" and "up there in heaven" to express the mystery of the two worlds cannot today be understood in a purely spatial sense, as they may well have been in the Jewish or Greek culture. Calvin's doctrine of the Eucharist, an attempt to safeguard at once the reality of Christ's presence and the historicity of his ascension into heaven, is strongly influenced by conceptions of space due to the cosmology of his day. It would be absurd today to oppose to Catholic doctrine on the real presence the same objections which Calvin advanced. One could go on multiplying examples of this kind to show how diversity of cultures obliges the tradition of the Gospel to distinguish sanely between the eternal truth, which must be transmitted, and its limited theological expressions, which must be changed since they are the result of the culture of one age and one region, and of a metaphysics relative to the developments of science.

The catholicity of the Church in space, then, requires the Church to introduce into her elaboration of the tradition of the Gospel the voices of various human cultures, differing in accordance with diversity of places and races.

TRADITION, DOXOLOGICAL UNDERSTANDING OF SCRIPTURE

True to *its priestly ministry,* the Church in its liturgy sustains a dialogue with God the Father, through Christ, in the Holy Spirit.

Holy Scripture makes up in large part the language of the Church in its liturgy. God speaks to it in the Scriptures; and by the words of the Scriptures, by the Psalms, by prayers woven of biblical language, it replies to God in praise and in supplication, in thanksgiving and in intercession. In the celebration of the sacraments, its life is concretely the Word of God which provides its nourishment.

Through this abundant use of the Scriptures in the liturgy, the Church in a certain manner makes a living experience of the Word of God; and this experience is an essential form of tradition.

In its choice of biblical texts for the liturgy, then, the Church provides a living interpretation of the Scriptures. The liturgy thus becomes a chief form of the catechesis. The connection established between such and such a psalm, or prophecy, or epistle, or gospel, or antiphon and such and such a feast or Sunday of the liturgical cycle indicates the spiritual exegesis which the Church makes of this text, and places it in a living relationship with the mystery of Christ. Thus we may say that the Church produces a living liturgical interpretation of the Scriptures. Naturally, this understanding is based upon the historical sense of the Bible; but it builds upon it further in applying the Word of God to the living actuality of salvation in the Church.

Thus the liturgy, therefore, and quite particularly the liturgies of the early centuries of the Church, make up an important part of the tradition of the Gospel. In the formulas of its official prayer, in the choice of texts and the composition of prayers, the early Church reveals to us its profound understanding of Revelation and transmits to us its faithful interpretation of the Gospel.

Furthermore, thus experienced dramatically in the liturgical mystery, the Word of God grows to be familiar in all its aspects to Church members accustomed to it in their prayer. Through both its choice of the texts used and its setting of them, the Church gives a universal and authentic interpretation of the Scriptures; but moreover, through living the life of this liturgy, Church members progressively assimilate the Word of God in all its richness and explore it in all its depth. This progressively keener understanding of the Scriptures in the liturgical life is also a form of tradition.[28]

The liturgy is the Church's ordinary form of proclaiming the truth. The redemption, the sacrifice of the cross and the victory of the resurrection, for example, have never had any other forms of proclamation than the liturgy with its annual cycle, its feasts, its biblical texts, its credos, its traditional prayers, and the preaching which accompanies it. The Church has made the mystery of Christ the Savior and his redemptive work its life, through the liturgy, without ever a council's having to make a pronouncement on this mystery in a dogmatic definition.

Thus, so long as a theological problem does not create a crisis in the Church and oblige it to summon a council and give a pronouncement, the faithful tradition of the Gospel continues to be accomplished by means of the liturgical life; the Church, that is, proclaims the truth in the process of glorifying its Lord; its theology is essentially doxological. In this attitude of adoration in the presence of God and attention to his Word, the universal Church receives from the Holy Spirit the correct interpretation of

[28] Cf. Y. M.-J. Congar, *La Tradition et les traditions, essai historique* (Paris: Arthème Fayard, 1960), pp. 86–91.

the Scriptures. But this is true of the Church universal and catholic. That is to say, the faithful tradition of the Gospel takes place through the liturgy in proportion as that liturgy is really universal, really catholic, in the line of the catholic prayer of the Church, and contains the fulness of faith and adoration inherited from the early Church. Uniformity, of course, is not necessary in Christian liturgies; but amidst their diversity they must display a biblical and catholic relationship, must draw from the fountains of the first centuries if they are to be authentic vehicles of the faithful transmission of the Gospel and enable the Church to experience profoundly the Word of God.

It is clear that outside situations of crisis when the Church has had to meet in councils to affirm truth against error, the faithful transmission of the Gospel has operated through the liturgy. The Church Fathers of the early centuries did their best teaching in the liturgical catecheses. There they explained the mystery of Christ, in a form more doxological than systematic. They aided the faithful to live with Christ in the liturgy. The early tradition of the Church, then, was essentially doxological and liturgical. Indeed, this doxological quality clings even to the definitions of the councils. They were liturgical texts and terms suited for divine worship rather than theological or metaphysical formulations. Such expressions as "God of God, Light of Light, true God of true God, begotten not made, consubstantial with the Father . . ." or "theotokos," for example, seem destined rather for turning the eyes of adoration towards the truth than for giving a logical exposition of the mystery. Yes, the most authentic tradition of the early Church is—outside the councils—conveyed in the pages of such works as St. Ambrose's *De Sacramentis* and *De Mysteriis,* and in the homilies and liturgical catecheses of the various Greek and Latin Fathers.

Even afterwards, when the intellectual life of the Church became more systematic, it is to the liturgy first of all that we must turn to find its authentic interpretation of the Scriptures. It is beyond doubt that the various liturgies maintained this understanding of the Scriptures with greater fidelity than did the various theological systems both of the Middle Ages and of modern times. To choose an example to be found in the Churches born of the Reform, the liturgical books—and the hymns in especial—did preserve accurately the doctrine of salvation, while many theologians, and even some Churches, were falling into liberalism and moralism.

Here we must direct attention to the tradition of the Orthodox and other Eastern Churches, which have succeeded better than the Western Churches in giving the pre-eminent place to the liturgy in the transmission of the Gospel. It might be said that all the Orthodox Church's teaching is to be found in its liturgy. In the East, the liturgy is conceived of as a world, the world of God, in which the worshiper lives, and moves, and contemplates the truth. The liturgical cycle, the feasts, and the sacraments give him all he needs to know to live as a Christian. There is no separation between liturgy and moral doctrine; the whole of Christian life is found in the liturgy; indeed, the whole of Christian life *is* liturgy. The tradition of the Gospel is conveyed quite naturally by the liturgy for the Orthodox Church; in the liturgy is to be found the authentic understanding of the truth revealed in the Scriptures and expressed and summarized by the councils.

Liturgy seeks the aid of art—and art, too, can be a form of tradition, a doxological understanding of the Scriptures. When the service of the Church's cult leads an artist to produce a creation expressing the glory of God and his people's praise of him, when the artist submits faithfully to the truth contained in the Sacred Scriptures (while preserving the full liberty of the requirements of his craft), he can be an instrument in the accurate transmission of the Gospel through the liturgy. He is the instrument whereby the truth incarnate in Jesus Christ comes into contact with the material world of forms, colors, and sounds. From this contact of the Gospel and created matter there emerges a species of objective correlative; and if truth finds here a contemporaneous form of expression, it may be effectively brought home to contemporary man. Thus the artist places at the disposition of the Gospel the instrument of his artistic creation so that the ageless truth may in his own age find means of expressing itself through the medium of forms, colors, and sounds in the liturgical celebration.

Here we must distinguish between art which is simply of religious inspiration and art designed to aid the liturgy or prayer. It is liturgical art properly speaking which, through its obedience to truth and its orientation towards worship, can be a vehicle of the transmission of the Gospel. We find very fine examples of this liturgical art as an instrument of tradition in the medieval Russian icons, in the windows, porticoes, and capitals of the old cathedrals, and in the frescoes of a Giotto or of a Fra Angelico. . . . And modern liturgical art is in the process of discovering new expressions of this Gospel tradition.

We have seen how the Church at Nicaea in 787, at the time of the seventh ecumenical council, acted against the iconoclasts and intended to emphasize the lawfulness of the use of images in divine worship. In this council the Church showed the ultimate consequences of Christology—of the dogma of the incarnation. Images symbolize the fact that the whole of creation, matter included, can be penetrated by Christ and can become signs of the presence of the Kingdom of God in our world: can cast a reflection of the eternal Light. The images of liturgical art are also lawful instruments of the authentic tradition of the Gospel in proportion as they express the truth faithfully and lead the people of God to true adoration, and in proportion as they are not mere decoration but a component of the Church's liturgy.

Thus, the traditional liturgy of the Church, through its utilization of the Scriptures, through the chants and prayers which sprang from its biblical reading and its dogma, and through its images, bears within itself the faithful tradition of the Gospel. At the same time, the liturgy permits us to discern how the Church understood the Scriptures during the course of the centuries, and is a means for the ecumenical reading of the Scriptures. But the emphasis of the liturgy is upon a doxological interpretation of these Scriptures; it utilizes them for praise of the Lord; it makes of them the place where God is to be listened to and adored—listened to in a spirit of adoration and adored with obedience. Thus the liturgy gives the Scriptures an interpretation perfectly adequate to them, for the Bible is not a scientific text affording us solutions for our intellectual problems, but the revelation of the almighty and merciful God gathering together his people for worship and service—for the liturgy and the Church's mission.

The Church never better understands the truth revealed in the Scriptures than when it has engaged in prayer in order to adore God and to intercede for all men. The liturgy, doxological comprehension of the Scriptures, is thus a privileged place where the

Church meets the truth and makes it the substance of its life. To sum up then, the liturgy is an essential form of the faithful tradition of the Gospel.

TRADITION, MISSIONARY UNDERSTANDING OF SCRIPTURE

Faithful to *its prophetic ministry,* the Church—which is essentially missionary—engages in a constant discussion with the world. This is not simply the world outside itself, to which it brings the Gospel which it has conscientiously meditated upon in the inner fastnesses of its theological and community life. The Church is holy but it bears within itself all the weary weight of the world, with its problems, its difficulties, and its sufferings: its temptations and its sin—these, too, it knows, in the person of the members which constitute its body. The preaching of the Gospel, then, begins inside, not outside, the Church.

Furthermore, if Scripture is unchangeable, it still must be preached in a way that will be understandable and that will make it effective. If it is to be so, no vague and superficial knowledge of the world to which it must bring the Gospel will suffice to prepare the Church for its work. For this reason, preaching the Gospel involves more than the unilateral action of the Church upon the world. The Church, to be sure, brings God's light to the world; but the world also brings to the Church information about how that light must be cast if the world is to be really enlightened.

The further advantage of this mutual understanding is that the Church, by making timely changes in the ways in which it projects the timeless and unchanging light, also learns more about the manifold qualities and potentialities of the light itself. In other words, when the Church succeeds in bringing the changeless Gospel to bear upon the multitudinous vicissitudes of the world, the Gospel—rising, so to speak, to the occasion—reveals its possession of previously undetected depths and breadths of truth. It is through the process of obliging the Church to make itself understood to the world, then, that the Holy Spirit—as Christ promised—leads the Church into all truth.

The Church reaches an understanding of itself in the process of conversing with the world. The Church, of course, does not learn its truths from the world; but it does find in it the men—all of them—for whom Christ died and whom it must reach if it is to realize Christ's own catholic amplitude. Christ's truth is indeed in the Gospel, but since it is there as directed to the world and not solely to the Church, what renders it clear is the Church's conversation with the world. In the very effort to understand the present-day world and to find the words and images that the world, in turn, will understand, the Church enriches its own understanding of the Scriptures.

Furthermore, Christ's governance extends to the whole world and to the men in it, whom he is mysteriously preparing to meet him. The Church, therefore, must not only be acquainted with Revelation, but must also be attentive to the signs of this mysterious preparation.

And then, the Church's conversation with the world can be a form of tradition since it is the basis of the Church's *present-day* understanding of the Gospel. This revelation of the contemporaneous relevance of the Gospel is thus another force extending the Church to its catholic amplitude.

When the Church encountered the Greek world and its philosophies the result was not an addition of new truths to biblical revelation. Everything had already been given the Church by the apostles in their inspired tradition of the Gospel. Nevertheless God, whose rule in the world is limitless, presided over this encounter. Through the Holy Spirit he assisted the Church so that in its contact with Greek thought it would choose the vocabulary most understandable to the world and least perilous to the truth.

Moreover, since Christ died for *all* men, so that *all* might attain truth and salvation, the Holy Spirit showed the Church on which side men were to be approached and in what way they might be disposed to receive the Gospel. He charted the mission for it, indicating where it was to go, for he himself was preparing the hearts of future Christians. For example, St. Paul had a vision of a Macedonian, who begged him to come to Macedonia: "That vision once seen," the compiler of the Acts wrote, "we were eager to sail for Macedonia; we concluded that God had called us there to preach to them" (Acts 16:10). When St. Paul was in Athens, he saw in the altar to the unknown god which had been erected by the Greeks a preparation for his preaching of the true God. "It is this unknown object of your devotion that I am revealing to you" (Acts 17:23).

Are we allowed to say that the worth-while things of this world are nought but the result of sin? They may be mysterious preparations of the Creator and Lord of all, which predispose men to receive the Gospel. It is from those sources that the Church must draw its vocabulary if it is to make the Word of God—intended for all—current among men. What if this Word does prove disruptive of human habits of thought? It will already have penetrated them in their worth-while aspects—those aspects, namely, of which the Lord of the world himself has promoted the development with an eye to the universal proclamation of the Gospel and to its reception by all men. Both the world's worth and the world's words, then, lend new richness to the preaching of the truth and world-wide currency to the Gospel. Constantly, then, does this meeting of Church and world afford the Church new viewpoints both in its understanding of Scripture and in its imparting of the Word of God. We repeat, all this has no effect on the content itself of the Gospel, but only displays the catholicity and richness of that content which in every time and place proves itself adaptable to new forms of expression for the salvation of all men.

The Church, therefore, must know the world; and to do so, it must be very much *in* the world. There is, after all, such a thing as a Docetist preaching of the Word of God, preoccupied with exegesis and the pure proclamation of the Gospel, with no attention to a real meeting with men and the world as they are. Often, undertaking the Christian mission and preaching the Gospel have meant a very praiseworthy confidence in the Bible's efficacy in itself, but a rejection of any consideration of the values and vocabulary of the world. Such a proclamation of the truth is not an authentic tradition of the Gospel. It simply uproots man from his social and human conditions and even more often risks reaching only the already uprooted.

If a real transmission of the Gospel is to take place, if the living Word of God is really to penetrate men and the World as they are today, the Church must be really present in the world, among men. It must, by living in the midst of them, grow to understand them as they are. It must take an interest in the interests and in the modes of expression of its day, the latter including not only words and metaphors, but the novels, the moving pictures, the plays—in a word, the literature of the day.

The Church must view as worth-while all these modern techniques of communication and give them optimistic acknowledgment. Sometimes the Church takes a pessimistic and puritanical attitude towards the world. If it is right in shunning and condemning sin in all its forms—war, injustice, cupidity, arrogance, which all use the values of this world for their own purposes—it must take a positive and hopeful attitude towards these values as they are in themselves, and consider sanctifying them for use for the Gospel's purposes. The conversation of the Church—joyously and peaceably present in the world and interested in all its values—with present-day man whose language it understands and speaks, offers a magnificent opportunity for the Gospel to find new means for expressing itself and thus revealing its catholicity and its effectiveness. The world—and what the Lord fosters in it as authentically worth-while—thus contributes to the faithful tradition of the Gospel which in every age reveals the richness of its treasures.

THE AGENTS OF TRADITION

Faithful to *its kingly ministry,* the Church is endowed with authority, sign of Christ's authority over it and over the world. We have seen how the apostles sent out by Christ were conscious of and exercised this authority. Because of the geographical extension of the Church and of its mission, they delegated their authority to certain ministers—overseers or elders. At last, feeling their end to be near they provided themselves with successors. These successors of the apostles could not take the exact place of the apostles for this was a unique one, designated by Christ; but they could carry on, in their name and with them, the ministry of unity and authority in the Body of Christ.

The Lord alone has full authority over his Body, the Church; with his apostles he continues to exercise this authority. The successors of the apostles, in their mission of unity and authority in the bosom of the Church, were but living and concrete signs of that unique authority—yet they were necessary signs. They were the trustworthy men (2 Tim. 2:2) whom St. Paul described and whom he recommended that Timothy, in his turn, designate as his successors.

The fact to be considered is that, since the full understanding of the Gospel is impossible save in the catholic communion of the Church, since truth is found only in charity (Eph. 4:15), the ministry of unity and authority is necessary for the maintenance of truth in the Church—for the faithful transmission of the Gospel. St. Paul made provision for this ministry and charged his successor, Timothy, to make similar provision in his turn.[29]

These bishops—apostolic successors—had the responsibility of the faithful transmission of the Gospel. They had to watch over and safeguard the deposit of faith—to take care, that is, that the Sacred Scriptures be preached and taught, that the sacraments be celebrated, that ministers be ordained, that liturgical prayer take place, that the ecumenical creeds be inviolate, and that the authority of the ecumenical councils be maintained in the Church. They were the agents whereby the apostles continued to exercise their authority in the name of Christ by means of the Scriptures as understood in the universal communion of the Church.

These bishops did not possess this ministry of unity and authority in isolation. In their local Churches, it was with the whole college of presbyters and other ministers that they exercised it.[30]

Nevertheless, through the charism and the office proper to themselves, they were the ones responsible for the unity of the Church and might be led, in case of a critical situation in their Church, to take the personal responsibility of seeing to it that their ministry of authority was respected. Furthermore, they had the responsibility for communion with the bishops of all the local

[29] This very brief paragraph is only a reminder of what we discussed at greater length, earlier in this volume, concerning the ministries of the Church as agencies of tradition.

[30] Cf. the letters of St. Ignatius of Antioch: "Do nothing apart from the bishop and the presbyters . . . nothing is good save what is in common" (*Magn.* VII, 1).

Churches in the world. Councils both regional and ecumenical were special occasions, of course, for the concretization of this communion. After the early centuries of the Church, an episcopal primate was charged with watching over the unity of bishops and with making decisions in cases of crisis in an ecumenical council. To study the role of this episcopal primate, however, lies beyond the scope of this volume.

This ministry of unity and authority was exercised by the bishops essentially in function of the guardianship of the apostolic deposit of faith. The Gospel could not be accurately understood and authentically transmitted except in the unity of the whole Church; that was why it was necessary to maintain that unity. The bishop was really engaged in the service of the authority of Christ and of his apostles who maintained the Church in unity. He was the living and concrete sign of that unity-creating authority. It was, therefore, in total submission to Christ and the apostles—that is, through guardianship of the deposit of faith and the preaching of the Gospel—that he exercised his ministry.

The bishop, then, is essentially a minister of the Word of God and of the sacraments, by which he governs the Church to keep it in unity. He is in the apostolic succession inasmuch as he is the guardian of the apostolic deposit of faith, accurately transmits this deposit, and is in communion with the other bishops, as a sign of universal Church unity. It is on this level that any discussion of apostolic succession must take place; the consecration of bishops by other bishops is a sign of this universal communion, in the absence of which there can be no full comprehension of the Scriptures and only a partial transmission of the Gospel. The deposit of faith cannot be safeguarded and transmitted in its totality except by the universal college of bishops, in communion with one another, in collaboration with the presbyters and other ministers of the local Churches and in touch with the whole Christian people.

The present study on the subject of tradition draws attention to the extent that present-day ecumenical efforts and progress towards a unity of the Churches are essential to the full understanding of the Sacred Scriptures. At different periods in its history the Church has emphasized different aspects of its faith or its life. In the fourth and fifth centuries, it was necessary to give this emphasis to its affirmation of its trinitarian and Christological dogmas; in the sixteenth century, it was necessary to re-emphasize the full authority of the Word of God and the full sufficiency of grace. This follows from the very life of the Church and its mission in the world.

Today, ecumenical unity of all Christians is essential to the life and mission of each Church. The Churches must, together, find the special truth which will accomplish their reform and their unity.

As for the important problem of tradition, which has a direct connection with the problem of Church unity, the task is to find the direction in which a solution favorable to unity may be found. In conclusion, we may leave to the reflection of all who are interested in ecumenical unity the following three declarations:

1) The Church is the Body of Christ—the fulness of Him who is Fulness itself.

2) Christ and the apostles are united to the Church in such a way that they continue to exercise their authority there through a ministry instituted by them and in such a way that they carry on, through this ministry, the faithful guardianship of the deposit of faith and the authentic tradition of the Gospel.

3) Sacred Scripture cannot be totally comprehended save in the universal communion of all the Churches, assisted by the Holy Spirit, and with the intention of transmitting the Gospel to men of the present day.

Spiritual Conversion and Prayer for Unity

3 Spiritual Conversion and Prayer for Unity

In speaking of prayer for the unity of Christians, we first must recall that it is no different from ordinary Christian prayer and is thus necessarily and indissolubly bound, as all prayer is, with humility. We are not really praying unless we have this attitude of humility, this spirit of poverty which looks to God for everything and admits that man is naught, incapable by himself of any good. Prayer for the unity of Christians involves the other elements of Christian prayer as well: adoration, confession of sins, thanksgiving, and intercession.

It is adoration first of all. It is impossible to pray without placing ourselves in the presence of God, realizing that God is there, that he sees us, and hears us, and indeed grants us a hearing. And in the certainty of the presence of Almighty God, Father, Son, and Holy Spirit, the first step in our prayer for unity—as in any prayer—is adoration of him. This impulse of adoration is somehow awakened in us by the contemplation of God as one and threefold. When we begin to pray for unity, we must realize the presence of the thrice-holy God, perfectly one in three persons. Christ, when he prayed for unity (John 17), asked for his Church and for his disciples the unity which binds him to the Father. Thus it is fitting that our prayer for the visible unity of Christians begin with the contemplation of this unity of God in three persons. In our adoration we shall contemplate as well God the

Creator, the Lord who by his omnipotence, in his immensity, holds creation entirely together, causing by his governance the unity of the universe—the unity which, having been disturbed by man's sin, has been restored by Christ's sacrifice.

Thus, in adoring the Creator, we form an idea of the depth of his wisdom and his love which keep his numberless creatures existing together in an admirable order.

Adoration of God bears also upon the Son, upon Christ who died for all, who re-established the relationship between humankind and the Father, who by his sacrifice wrought unity, and who has enabled us to become once more the children of one and the same Father in one and the same family, the family of God. This family of the Father, invisible and known to him alone, extends immeasurably beyond the picket fences of our sometimes narrow ecclesiologies. Christ died for all men; in the vastness of the world, the Spirit breathes where he will. Contemplation of the Spirit directs our attention to the Lord who desires to be everywhere, to penetrate everything, in order to bring everything towards the perfect unity of the Kingdom. In our adoration we contemplate Christ the King, the Lord reigning truly over all men, whoever they are, to whatever religion they belong. The Church believes that mysteriously its Lord acts so as to bring together into the one fulness of the truth all God's children, scattered far and wide. The Church does not consider itself some kind of closed society, a club for the privileged. The Christian, living member of a truly universal Church, prays for an inclusive unity which will embrace all men.

The Christian prays that out of this troubling diversity of ideas, philosophies, and religions the Lord will draw to himself—that is, to the unity of his Body—the men nowadays divided in every quarter of the globe. Thus, in the act of adoring the Lord, the Christian embraces all humanity in his prayers for unity: he adores the unity of his one and threefold God and contemplates him as Lord of all this universe making its way towards the unity of the Kingdom.

Confession of sins also plays its part in the prayer for unity. For the fact is that Christ, when he founded his Church, wished it to be perfectly one. He prayed that the unity of Christians might be maintained; but the sin of humankind, their blindness, and their inability to discern the unity in their diversity—these led them to oppose one another and to become divided. Prayer for unity cannot be valid if it is not an act of humility wherein man confesses his responsibility in this division. It cannot be the result of a merely general feeling. This confession of sins commits us to real repentance, a new conversion. In this confession of our sin, this recognition of our responsibility in the division of Christians, there must be entailed a real change in our lives. Our prayer for unity leads us to a better obedience to Christ; it moves us to return to the fundamentals of our faith, to live them to the hilt in a charity which believes all things, hopes all things, and bears all things.

Our prayer for unity is also one of thanksgiving. We must thank God for having led men to this concern over lost unity. We must thank him for having put into the heart of increasing numbers of men both distress over their division and an ardent desire to leave no stone unturned in the quest for the reality of that unity—which does exist, and which we have but to learn to recognize and incorporate into our lives. We thank God for having raised up apostles of unity, pioneers who have devoted their lives and their ministry to this task. Finally, we thank God for the whole ecumenical movement and for all the fruits it has already borne today in the Church.

Our prayer for unity is also intercession, or supplication. More and more we must bring before God, with great confidence, all the present-day needs of divided Christians. Our intercession is in a way a sharing of our difficulties and our sufferings—a sharing which takes place in the presence of God as an appeal to him to heal this wound of our division. Thus our prayer for the visible unity of Christians has all the elements of every most simple Christian prayer. It is adoration, confession, thanksgiving, and intercession.

CHRIST'S PRAYER TO THE FATHER

If Christians pray for unity, it is because Christ gave them an example. On the even of his passion he prayed for the unity of his disciples. St. John's Gospel gives us a report of that prayer

(Chapter 17): "That they may all be one; that they too may be one in us, as thou, Father, art in me, and I in thee; so that the world may come to believe that it is thou who has sent me. And I have given them the glory which thou gavest to me, that they should all be one, as we are one; that while thou art in me, I may be in them, and so they may be perfectly made one. So let the world know that it is thou that has sent me, and that thou hast bestowed thy love upon them, as thou hast bestowed it on me."

The extraordinary thing about this prayer is that it is a real prayer; that is to say, it supposes a hearing but also a difficulty, a possibility that unity will in fact not be maintained. And yet Christ said: "I have given them the glory which thou hast given me, so that they may be one just as we are one." Christians in the Church partake of the glory of God. They are enlightened with his light, they are covered with his love, they are perfectly illuminated with his truth; and this should produce unity among them; Christ has affirmed it. He said moreover, "I in them and thou in me, so that they may be perfectly one." Christ continues to live with us; as he is one with the Father, so he is one with his Body, the Church.

How, then, when Christ has given so great fulness to his Church, when he has given us his glory, is it possible for this fulness and this glory to be compromised by division? Plainly, this is baffling; but there it is. Of course, there does exist a fundamental unity, an indefectible one, that the Church can never lose: this is the unity hidden in Christ. The Church is the Body of Christ and this Body cannot be divided. But in the concrete manifestations of the life of Christians, in the history of the Church in this world, the fact cannot escape us that division has compromised this fundamental unity and disguised it from view. Thus Christ, who forsaw this possible division at the same time as he gave his glory to his disciples so that they might be one, prayed to the Father to keep them in that unity.

The unity bestowed by Christ can be compromised, then, by men. It is possible to believe in a unity bestowed by God and at the same time to pray that this unity be sustained and be manifested. In fact, Christ himself contemplated the unity of his disciples—he had given them his glory in order that they might be one as the Father and he are one; and at the same time he prayed that they might in fact be one, so that the world would believe. Unity, then, is a fundamental reality, existing and subsisting in the Body of Christ; but Christians must nevertheless pray for their unity—pray that they themselves stay in this unity bestowed by Christ and, when they are divided, pray that the fundamental unity bestowed upon them in Jesus Christ may be rediscovered.

There is no opposition between the unity given and the unity to be looked for; unity is both—a gift and the object of a quest. This fact is what gives prayer for unity its dynamism. Prayer for unity is not a quest for something which does not exist and must be waited for like something yet to happen. Unity is given in Christ—there is one sole faith, one sole baptism, one sole Body of Christ—but at the same time this real unity, present in the Body of Christ, can be the object of an investigation, of a more searching study, of an ever more conscious realization.

Christ has given us an example of an unshakable certainty of unity which still does not keep one from praying for unity, so that this unity—already given, and quite real—may be manifested concretely, and may be a living unity. Thus a Christian may certainly believe that he belongs to the true Church, and believe that he knows the secret of real unity, and yet at the same time pray that this unity be not an exclusive one, but increasingly inclusive and rich in universal potentialities. We cannot judge such a Christian if he prays that others find the unity which he himself has discovered in his own Church, so long as in his prayer he makes room for unity's essential dynamism—as long, that is, as he is fully conscious that the unity in his Church is not a static one, a unity fixed once and for all, but a living unity which is daily enriched, daily brought further, daily enlarged towards the final unity of the Kingdom of God. In his prayer for unity, the Christian—like Christ on the eve of his passion—believes that the glory of the Father has been bestowed upon the Church and that the plenitude of truth is to be found in the communion of the universal Church; but at the same time he believes that this fundamental unity may expand and deepen; it is for this fundamental—yet expansive and progressive—unity that he prays.

In Christ's prayer, the unity of Christians, founded upon and inspired by the unity of the Father and the Son, is not an end in itself. If Christians are called upon to live in this unity provided for them by God, it is so that the world will believe—so that the world will know that the Father has sent the Son and that the Son has loved as the Father has loved him.

Herein we can more plainly see why unity is a reality that expands and is enriched in pace with the advance of history, our closer approach to the Kingdom of God, and the development of the world. As the ages pass, the Church must answer new questions; and as a rule it will not provide the world repeatedly with the same fixed solution; rather, the Holy Spirit who leads it into all truth causes it to realize progressively the countless riches of the Word of God, and the inestimable diversity involved in the unity of the Body of Christ.

Thus there is no contradiction between certainty that unity has been given us and prayer for progressively enriched unity. Like Christ's prayer, ours must ask essentially for Christians' discovery of the unity existing among Father, Son, and Holy Spirit, and their radical participation in the life of this unity so that the world may believe. Christians are not obliged to make other requests on this subject; they need not pray that unity be realized in such and such a particular way. Of course, they have the right to believe that there are certain fundamental conditions apart from which unity cannot exist. But when they pray, they are first and foremost bent in adoration before the Father, Son, and Holy Spirit; and their essential prayer is to ask that all Christians receive the grace to live in that divine unity, both actual and becoming.

PRAYER IN CHRIST THROUGH THE HOLY SPIRIT

We find in St. Paul (Rom. 8:24–27) this same dynamism of a prayer based on a reality fully given but seeking the fulfilment of that reality. Speaking of salvation, St. Paul declares: "Our salvation is founded upon the hope of something. Hope would not be hope at all if its object were in view; how could a man still hope for something which he sees? And if we are hoping for something still unseen, then we need endurance to wait for it." St. Paul believes with all his faith that a Christian is saved by the sacrifice of Christ. But if there is an element already *given* in the complex of salvation, there is also an element of *becoming;* and this element of becoming he sees in the travail of our bodies for redemption. Thus a Christian believes that he has been redeemed by the sacrifice of Christ, that he is dead and arisen with Christ in baptism, and that he has become a new creature. But he believes at the same time that there is room for prayer that this radical salvation progressively absorb his whole life and be completed at last, after long perseverance, in the reward of the Kingdom of God.

Continuing his train of thought, the Apostle adds: "Only, as before, the Spirit comes to the aid of our weakness; when we do not know what prayer to offer, to pray as we ought, the Spirit himself intercedes for us, with groans beyond all utterance: and God, who can read our hearts, knows well what the Spirit's intent is; for indeed it is according to the mind of God that he makes intercession for the saints." This text, applying as it does to every Christian prayer, can be applied to prayer for unity. In his life of prayer—prayer for unity included—a Christian does not know what to petition so as to pray as he ought. Of course, he may have some certainties on the subject of conditions for Church unity, but as we have seen fundamental Church unity is progressive, in the process of development; it continues to be enriched; and it is right here that a Christian recognizes his ignorance. He does not know what potentialities the unity of the Body of Christ possesses. So, in his prayer for unity, he submits to the Holy Spirit, recognizing his own human weakness, the poverty of his imagination, and his incapacity to comprehend God's plans. In the avowal of this weakness he calls upon the Holy Spirit for help. And the Holy Spirit himself makes the required intercession.

Our prayer cannot dictate a solution to God; but in asking aid of the Holy Spirit, we are asking that the words be given us and true prayer furnished us, so that passing via the will of Christ, it will reach the Father. And the prayer with which the Holy Spirit furnishes us is in line with God's outlook. The Holy Spirit's intercession through the Church does in fact intercede; the prayer which he places in our hearts and upon our lips rises infallibly to the Father through Christ. Any prayer genuinely submitted to the inspirations of the Holy Spirit in the Church is a prayer that Christ, our heavenly High Priest, makes his own, one to which the Father will surely grant a hearing.

Applied to prayer for unity, this way of praying is at the same time a summons to humility, to docility, as we recall with St. Paul that our prayer for unity cannot impose any ready-made solutions on God. There is no implication here of an abdication of our beliefs. We can believe in certain conditions necessary for the existence and maintenance of Christian unity; but this prayer —illuminated by, and so to speak under the proprietorship of, the Holy Spirit—is a perfectly docile one, bestowing upon us both confidence in God's aims and a disposition to execute them.

In this prayer by the Holy Spirit in Christ the High Priest, then, there is an act of confidence: the Lord, who knows all things, can accomplish the perfect unity of Christians to a point infinitely beyond anything we can imagine or desire. This prayer in Christ by the Spirit allows great scope for what we have already referred to as the dynamism of prayer. It is founded upon an act of faith, faith explicit and certain, but a faith capable of being enriched and expanded in the light of the Holy Spirit.

St. Paul teaches us complete docility of mind and heart in prayer for unity. Here more than in any other prayer we need to have our intercession for the faithful correspond with God's aims. We have no right to come between him and those aims; and the sole means for making sure that our prayer is in harmony with the actual designs of God is to enter in some way into Christ's prayer, by letting ourselves be directed by the Holy Spirit. And thus the Holy Spirit who breathes where he will and Christ who is the Church's High Priest, interceding unremittingly before the Father, will unify the very diverse prayers of Christians, making of them real prayer, for the real unity to which we look forward.

PRAYER OF THE CHURCH—ONE, HOLY, UNIVERSAL, AND APOSTOLIC

If our prayer for unity ascends to the Father in Christ the High Priest through the Holy Spirit, who gives us the power of genuine intercession, we must not forget that it is not an individual prayer but a prayer in the Church and of the Church. It is in communion with all our fellow Christians, incorporated with us by the same baptism in the Body of Christ, that we must offer up our prayer for unity, that is, in communion with the one, holy, universal, and apostolic Church, the Church militant and the Church triumphant, the Church of all places and all times.

First, then, we pray in communion with a Church that is one: our prayer for unity is not the prayer of groups of separated Christians who have never known unity and have to undertake together the building of an edifice which has never yet existed. Our prayer for unity is the prayer of the one Church, the undivided Church, the Church of the first centuries, the Church whose members in heaven know this perfect unity today. Thus we must be wholly disposed towards the unity already existing in the Body of Christ when we say our prayer. What we have to pray for, of course, is that this unity will become manifest; and we must believe that this underlying unity *will* manifest itself in a unique arrangement which God is preparing for us, in his great mercy and despite the sin of our division. The Christian unity which our prayer implores will not be some kind of compromise, some more or less successful shift, but the rediscovery by our presently myopic minds of the perfect and visible unity which the Body of Christ enables us to live in faith from now on.

Secondly, our prayer for unity is also the prayer of a Church which is holy: we believe that our unity will be founded upon the holy things which the Master has left us as treasures to be safeguarded. We must pray, then, to understand the Sacred Scriptures better, to have minds and hearts ever more faithfully submitted to the fulness of truth contained in the Word of God. We must pray to be ever more really and concretely nourished by the sacraments which the Lord in his goodness has transmitted to us. We must pray to rediscover our unity in the life provided by our baptism, and by our Eucharist. There is but one baptism; and in this baptism which has made us members of Christ's Body we must look to find our unity. We are separated in our communion of the Body and Blood of Christ; and yet it is in the Sacred Banquet that we meet our Lord Jesus Christ, really present. Our prayer must petition that the separation of our Eucharists become ever more clearly a temporary thing, making us long for the time when it will be given us to sit down all together in the evening at the table in the real presence of Jesus Christ. Our prayer for unity is also the prayer of a holy Church because it is the prayer of holy people—the saints. All who fought the good fight of faith are now at rest with God, awaiting the resurrection. They experience perfect unity; in the communion of saints we must join in with those countless multitudes and ask of God the unity—manifold and perfect—which they already know.

Thirdly, our prayer for unity is the prayer of a Church which is universal, spread throughout the whole world. It must be open to all the rich Christian developments on the face of the earth. Our thought in our prayer must not be that unity will be achieved through the victory of one limited tradition in the Church over other—presumed inferior—traditions. What we must wish for is the real unity of all Christians of every race, of every land, of every tradition, of every liturgy. This does not mean some hugger-mugger of anything and everything which has lived and now exists among Christians in their miscellaneous differences and divisions. If they are to regain unity, Christians will have to give up everything that is fractional and partisan in their outlook and in their traditions. But unity will come about through a mighty integration of all worth-while acquisitions, the riches resulting from all that has been authentically experienced by all Christians the world over. Our prayer for unity, then, asks for our personal enrichment and for the enrichment of our Church by everything which has been part of authentic Christian life everywhere under the sun.

Fourthly, our prayer for unity is the prayer of a Church which is apostolic. For we asked to be enriched in heaping measure not only by the life of the Church in all places, but also by the life of the Church in all ages, which go back, of course, to the apostles. Our prayer for unity asks for full communion with what the apostles believed, what the martyrs concretely lived, and what the Church's doctors taught. Our unity cannot be a simply contemporaneous one; our prayer for unity cannot ask simply that the whole past be forgotten and that under the pressure of modern times Christians acquire a smart and thrifty unity while wrinkling up their noses at history. In each age the Church has turned some facet of Revelation square to the light; and we must be aware of our solidarity with this wide experience of the Church's through the ages. A Christian—believe though he may that he is now living in the true Church, which knows true unity—must consider that this Church and this unity are bound to an immense past—to a line of God's people stretching back through history. The unity which we ask for in our prayer is a unity rich and living, which goes on abuilding and expanding, the unity of a people on the march, of a people who acquire and have acquired in every century, in every age, a new experience of the life of God.

PRAYER OF THE CHURCH EN ROUTE TO THE KINGDOM

1) *Christ's return, and the judgment*

In our prayer for unity we must keep in view the coming again of Christ, and the last judgment. Lacking this eschatological side, our prayer may be self-centered, a prayer which dictates to God an immediate settlement, already forseen in all its details. If, in contrast, our prayer is dominated by hope for the second coming of Christ and by the penumbra of the last judgment, then we have a vantage from which we can see beyond the familiar present-day situation of the Church as we understand it. When Christ returns he will not separate Church from Church—if Christians are then still misfortunately divided—but will distinguish in every Church between those who belong to him and those who have denied him. Even if a Christian believes that he belongs to the true Church and knows what is true unity, he is aware that upon the second coming judgment may rest on him and his brothers in the faith for irresponsible use of the gift that has been given them.

Thus, whatever our confidence in our unity and in our Church, thoughts of Christ's return and of the judgment recall us to humility; and they permit us to recognize Christians separated from us as authentic children of God: whatever the shortcomings we may find in their Church life, they believe in Christ as the Savior, they are baptized and incorporated into the Body of Christ, they receive the food of his presence, and, upon his return, they too will enter the Kingdom of God.

2) *Dogmatic development*

The Church is progressing towards the Kingdom not only in its concrete life but also in the increasingly rich understanding it receives of the Word of God. Through the Holy Spirit dwelling in it, the Church acquires an ever better understanding of the revelation contained in Sacred Scripture. The quest for the fulness of truth leads to ever deeper penetration of the Lord's message to his Church.

To be sure, the Church has been led, in certain great ecumenical meetings such as the general councils, to give definition to what it has discoverd in the Word of God, and though these decisions of the one Church, assembled in council, have an authority which is not equivalent to that of the Scriptures, still they represent an authentic and enduring interpretation of revealed data. At the same time, the Church's thought has always been that from one council to another council, from one universal interpretation of the truth to another such interpretation, progress may take place; not that the Church may contradict itself and see in the Scriptures something contrary to what it saw there in the early councils; but in the sense that a truth perceived in a council may become more explicit, may expand, may loom larger in the consciousness of the Church.

Thus the Church, at the Council of Ephesus, after having defined the full divinity of Jesus Christ present in his humanity and the perfect unity of this divinity and this humanity, was brought some time afterwards, at the Council of Chalcedon, to emphasize the *distinction* between these two natures in Christ—the divine nature and the human nature. There was no contradiction between the one council and the other, but if the Council of Chalcedon had not taken place the definitions of the Council of Ephesus might have degenerated into heresy, though they were true in themselves.

Thus there has been a dogmatic development throughout the history of the Church and the history of the councils; the Church is not static in its mental life, nor even in its dogmatic proclamations. When the Church reaches the point in the course of a council to deny an error and to define the truth contained in the Sacred Scripture, that solemn declaration is binding on the whole Church, but is binding on it until, in a new council and in a new definition, what has today been affirmed and formulated expands, develops, and becomes more explicit and hence more absolute, more close to the thought of God.

In this connection, the idea has not gone unexpressed that the definitions of the first Vatican Council, in 1870, on the subject of the authority and infallibility of the Pope, might perhaps find a more explicit formulation, a new comprehension, in the Second Vatican Council, which has been convoked by John XXIII. Through definition of the role of a council—the role of the bishops in communion with one another and with the bishop of Rome—there may come about a further clarification of the authority of the Pope as defined by the first Vatican Council. At any rate, we must hope that in the Second Vatican Council the doctrine of the Church is formulated in such a way that ecumenical discussions of the future may become even more fruitful.

This conception of dogmatic development in the course of council history permits a kind of prayer not exclusively directed to the conversion of all Christians to the dogmas today defined by one part of Christianity. In fact, whatever our ecclesiological situation, we are permitted to hope that some dogmas—defined though they be in the most solemn manner—may acquire in a new council (even one which does not unite all Christians) a further formulation such as will provide a basis for more adequate ecumenical conversations—and, finally, unity.

Prayer for unity may thus petition that such and such a dogma that today interposes an obstacle to unity may be so explained that, having better clarification, it may receive better understanding than it did in the past. Here again we meet the dynamic conception of prayer for unity, which does not have in view simply the acceptance of some ecclesiastical or dogmatic position which has been definitively gained, and remains static, but rather a prayer which has in view a common progress towards a greater light. This prayer for unity, looking forward to God's tomorrow, may therefore licitly ask for a real and profound conversion on the part of all Christians to the truth which is in Christ Jesus, the truth which he wishes to see accepted by his whole Church.

MAJOR COMMON INTENTIONS OF PRAYER FOR UNITY

1) *Invisible unity*

Although we are separated into different Churches which do not profess the same faith nor participate in the same sacrament of the Eucharist, an invisible unity exists among us which no one can deny. This invisible unity is the unity of the Body of Christ in which we have been incorporated by baptism; this invisible unity is nourished by the Holy Spirit, poured out at Pentecost and operative today in all the divisions of Christianity. We can pray for this interior unity, this unity in Christ within the single family of the Father and the communion of the Holy Spirit, to be deepened and enriched. This prayer for invisible unity imposes no a priori condition. Every Christian, whatever his Church affiliation, believes that beyond the limits set by his Church the Lord is preparing hearts for himself which will one day be united in the same faith and will participate in the same sacrament. Our prayer for unity may thus find its rationale in this great spiritual family, which unites in all the Churches those who have set their foot in the way of the Kingdom of God and henceforth live by the salvation given in Jesus Christ.

This prayer for invisible unity embraces without distinction the whole world. Our Lord asked that we might be one so that the world would believe. God—in his great mercy and in his providence—does not abandon any single man on earth. Step by step he leads every man to a meeting with Christ. Towards every single man on earth, then, all Christians have a grave responsibility. Our prayer for unity embraces all men, and presents them to God so that in their meeting with Christ they shall not be scandalized by our divisions, our intransigence, our narrowness.

2) *Visible unity in Scripture and Baptism*

We must acknowledge with thankfulness the immense privilege all Christians have of believing that God's revelation is handed down to them in one and the same Sacred Scripture. Not counting some secondary and limited details, all Christians do recognize the same Holy Scriptures: this is a sign that the Holy Spirit resolves to keep scattered Christians within a fundamental unity. Our prayer for unity must ask that this visible unity in the Scriptures become ever more real. Our prayer will ask from the Lord a biblical revival, developing further and further in the Churches. We can already see the immense progress of this biblical revival in our century; but it is still needful that both Churches and faithful express their faith more and more in the language of the Bible. Thus will this fundamental unity which we possess in the corpus of the Scriptures deepen and become more tangible, more appreciable.

Another common intention in our prayer for unity is the further development by each Christian of the grace received in baptism.

There is but one sole baptism in the name of the Father, and of the Son, and of the Holy Spirit, whatever be the Church that celebrates it. Since God has given us the grace to maintain among ourselves this further sign of our visible unity, separated though we be, it is up to us to try to live up to this sacrament better and better in our divided Christian life.

As St. Paul wrote to the Romans (Chapter 6), we have passed in baptism through death and resurrection in Christ. If we believe that, we must reflect that all our fellow Christians are beneficiaries of the death and resurrection of Christ, that they live a new life, and that they are incorporated in Christ and in the communion of the Holy Spirit. Our prayer for unity can ask for all Christians the renewal in them of this mystery of incorporation in Christ, and their ever closer attachment to their Lord. We can pray for the sanctification of all separated Christians whatever their Church affiliation—the sanctification of which the Holy Spirit, given in baptism, is the author.

If the grace of baptism assures all Christians of a life in Christ, a life in the Holy Spirit, we must reflect that this life affects the very existence of the various Churches. The separated Churches are composed of baptized members incorporated in Christ and in the communion of the Holy Spirit. Our prayer, based upon this certainty, will ask for the life of these Churches to be renewed by the presence of these baptized persons who wish to live a life consistent with their baptism. How vast the hope we may have as we see the faithful of all the Churches, and their priests or pastors, and their hierarchies! Whatever judgment may bear upon particular individuals, we must cast into the scales this hope that the power of baptism can renew all Christians, wherever they are; and this, too, is the object of an intention common to all Christians.

3) *Visible unity in prayer and faith*

It is also a grace that all Christians have in common the possession of the Our Father and of the Psalms for their prayers. When we say the Lord's Prayer, we should recall that it is the prayer of us all, that its petitions are uttered in every quarter of the globe by all Christians. We can make of the Our Father a real prayer for unity and ask that this prayer, handed down to us by our Lord himself, become verified on the lips of all Christians. Thus, when we ask: "Forgive us our trespasses as we forgive those who trespass against us"—or, in a more exact translation—"Forgive us our debts, as we forgive our debtors," we must have in mind, in this petition, solicitude for our divisions and the intention of our Christian unity. We may feel that our separated brothers are indebted to us, that they owe us brotherly love, respect, and consideration. Even if they fail to accord us these, we must bring ourselves to remit them that debt, forget the damage they do, no longer take account of it, and persevere in ecumenical intention—in prayer for unity.

All Christians use the Psalms as prayers. We can make of the Psalms, too, a prayer for unity. Such of them as condemn evil, sin, the Enemy, we can use as prayers of exorcism against whatever might injure Christian unity in its progress towards reunion in a single Church. Such as praise the Lord and thank him for his great wonders, we can use as prayers of praise of all that the Lord has done today to favor the reunion of Christians. Psalms of the sick or of the despairing we can recite as the sick among God's people and as folk without hope save in their Lord, only true guide along the paths of Christian unity.

Our prayer for unity must give thanks as well for the fact that there have been maintained, throughout the whole history of the Church and despite divisions, the fundamental truths of our Christian faith. The greater part of Christians profess their faith in the words of the Nicene and Apostles' Creeds. We must pray that these summaries of faith will continue to flourish throughout the Church. Thus, in our progress towards unity, we can profess the same faith in the one and threefold God, the same faith in Christ the Savior, true God and true Man, and the same faith in the Holy Spirit, dwelling in the Church. Still another grace is the fact that the greater part of Churches recognize the authority of the first four ecumenical councils. We may ask for authority of these councils to be maintained, and for theologians to refrain from too great temerity in their judgment on the thought of the Fathers of the Church, who were the first to read the Scriptures, to live by them, and to interpret them for the upbuilding of the Church.

4) *Progress of visible unity in the ecumenical movement*

The ecumenical meeting of minds which has become manifold in our century is a grace for which we are at a loss for words in which to thank God. All of us ought to be sensible to the marrow of our debt of gratitude here, and moved to beseech God that such contacts will be truly inspired and guided by the Holy Spirit.

This is something new in the history of the Church, something unique, for Christians to seek to draw close to one another as they are doing today. How careful must we be that in our own conception of unity, in our own prayer for unity, we do not risk compromising this ecumenical movement. Very naturally, from the fact of our various Church affiliations, we are going to have our particular notion of Church unity; but before advancing it too categorically, we must pray and we must ponder so that the Holy Spirit will subtilize our vocabularies and our psychologies so as to enable us to speak to our brothers without wounding them and without jeopardizing a common aspiration for the unity of all.

It is certain that the ecumenical movement of the non-Roman Churches is a fruit of the Spirit. Ever more clearly he delineates an image of what a fraternal communion among Christians might amount to—Christians who accept one another in their differences. The World Council itself has declared expressly that it is not a "super-Church," and does not aim to assure an authority not recognized in it by the Churches. It is based on no one particular notion of the Church and it is not prepared to prejudge the solution of the ecclesiological problem. Nor does it require that any member Church modify its own ecclesiological conceptions. In a word, there is nothing about it that requires any one specific conception of the nature of the unity towards which we are progressing.

This wise position of the World Council's permits every Christian and every Church attached to it to pray sincerely. The Churches do not have to give up their convictions; but they may hope for a ripening of these through contacts with their separated brethren. One of the intentions of the prayer for unity is for all the Churches of the World Council steadily to acquire a spirit of sacrifice as regards the unnecessary particulars of their traditions for the sake of reunion in one sole Church of Christ. But at the same time, the prayer for unity must ask that none of these Churches feel itself inferior and believe itself obliged to disappear in order to allow some other Church to carry the day; for it is in brotherly exchange, mutual illumination, and mutual respect that the way to Christian unity lies.

The convocation in our day of the second ecumenical Vatican Council provides our prayer with matter for thanksgiving. That the Pope set up a secretariat to take care of participation of non-Catholics in the council is something over which we must rejoice. It is a fruit of all the work accomplished by the pioneers of the ecumenical movement within the Catholic Church. We must thank God for having raised up such men within the Roman Church and for allowing more definite ecumenical work to be carried on today in Rome itself. That there will be difficulties—without doubt—is but a reason for us to implore the Holy Spirit to come upon this work.

Our prayer for unity must not ask that the Roman Catholic Church become something different from what it fundamentally is; we do not have the right to hope that Christians separated from us will be led to renounce their faith; but our prayer for unity, in invoking the coming of the Holy Spirit upon the ecumenical movement in Catholicism, may ask that the Roman Church may become more and more truly Catholic, opening itself to all the ecclesiastical riches of this great globe.

5) *Unity of the ministry.*

Everyone knows that in our ecumenical contacts we are forever running up against this problem of the Church's ministry. Certain Churches cannot recognize the full validity of the ministry in some other Churches. And for many of us this is very painful. The fact is that when a man has received a calling from his Lord, and when, after fitting himself for it in accordance with the preparation provided by his Church, he exercises the ministry of the Word and of the sacraments, it is not going to be easy for him to watch the validity of what he has accomplished being placed in doubt.

No, our prayer for unity at this point should become urgent that the Churches may discover, through a searching consideration of theology and history, the possibility of expressing the unity of all the ministrations carried on in the name of the Lord Jesus Christ, and that they inquire also into the possibility of reuniting all ministries in a sacramental communion required by the visible Church. A great breadth of conception in the Holy Spirit is called for here. In fact, we cannot speak simply of valid ministries or invalid ministries; we must look to the Lord who calls men to serve him in the proclamation of the Gospel and in prayer. And in this contemplation of the Lord of vocations, the Holy Spirit will give us perhaps the key to the unity of various ministries in the various separated Churches.

PARTICULAR CONVICTIONS AND PRAYER FOR UNITY

We have just reviewed the chief common intentions of prayer for unity, that is, what we may ask for truly in common without betraying our fidelity to our belief and our Church. Now we are going to try to understand how we may pray together for unity even though we have particular convictions which we cannot keep silent about without danger of being hypocrites. We are placing ourselves here in the perspective of a moderate opinion among the various Christian traditions—a perspective not necessarily that of any particular movement, group or community, which may not share the particular convictions expressed here.

1) *Protestant convictions*

We shall limit ourselves here to pointing out three specific convictions that distinguish the average Protestant outlook.

Given Protestantism's major premise—that the supreme and final authority in dogmatic and ecclesiastical matters is the Sacred Scriptures—it is certain that Protestants are going to hope that in all the Churches the Bible will be recognized as the sole final authority. Moreover, they are going to hope that ecclesiastical traditions, even the most venerable and the most solid, will be able to be called into question by the Churches in the light of the Sacred Scriptures; not in the light of the Sacred Scriptures understood in accord with a personal judgment, of course, but in the light of the Bible as read and understood in the communion of the universal Church. The average Protestant, brought up on this conception of the Bible as sole and sovereign authority, cannot not hope, deep down inside at least, that this authority will receive from all Christians the recognition he gives it himself.

To come now to the authority of the Pope and his infallibility: it is certain that Protestantism will not be able to get away from the idea that some day this doctrine of papal infallibility *(ex sese, non autem ex consensu Ecclesiae)* is going to have to be taken up again, restudied, and even corrected. One simply cannot picture a Protestant getting on his knees to pray that some day he may accept the dogma of papal infallibility. Even if a Protestant finds it in him to admit the primacy of a bishop like the bishop of Rome, in an ecumenical council; even if he can admit that in the case of a deadlock this primate may give a definitive decision, imposing his solution on the council; still, for this Protestant such solutions remain in some way provisory—stopgaps until unanimity is established in the Church. Thus your average Protestant cannot disregard a conviction that inclines him to hope that papal infallibility will be reconsidered.

As for Roman-Catholic mariology, the average Protestant who is not accustomed to making a place for the Virgin Mary in his piety will surely find it to his advantage to divest himself of an attitude too exclusively anti-Catholic. Nevertheless, he will find no room for docility towards doctrines he judges incompatible with his evangelical belief; he will hope that mariological development in the Roman Church will undergo some restraint, and that the importance Marian piety has assumed will become gradually tempered and brought back within the limits which seem to him conformable to the New Testament.

In giving expression here to these Protestant convictions which will play a conscious or unconscious part in prayer for unity, it has not been our aim to wound Catholic feelings in these matters.

In fact, prayer for unity is impossible if unaccompanied by great respect for the belief of our separated brethren. If we have thought it opportune to point out just what these average Protestant convictions are and to indicate that they will persist consciously or unconsciously in the hearts of the faithful of the Churches born of the Reform when they pray for unity, it is rather to show that—despite these convictions which seem to our Catholic brethren to go counter to their own particular certainties—prayer for unity still remains possible.

For what finally carries the day are the common intentions of all Christians who hope for the revitalization of all the Church, the full light of truth, and full charity among all Christians. Even with particular convictions, prayer for unity remains a prayer in Christ, submitted to the will of Christ and expressing readiness to accept whatever Christ wills. A Protestant would not be really faithful if he did not think that Christ wishes to lead him into all truth, even into a truth of which he is not here and now conscious. In this docility we find the true measure of prayer for unity. The believer remains receptive, and as it were surrenders to the work of the Holy Spirit in the whole Church. Such docility leaves him with all his hopes and is truly in the spirit of the petition of the Our Father: "Thy will be done."

2) *Catholic convictions*

Our Orthodox and Anglican brethren, Old Catholics as well with still others perhaps, can preserve in their prayer for unity the docility we have just spoken of in discussing Protestant convictions, but they cannot be faithful to their Church and their tradition without having convictions which are proper to themselves.

These "Catholic" Churches hold that unity cannot come about except through mutual acceptance among Churches of one and the same ministry. They think that this one and only ministry is in some way guaranteed and authenticated by episcopal ordination. The ministry is not, for them, fully valid in the universal Church unless ingrafted there by episcopal ordination in the apostolic succession (understood as the unbroken series of consecrations of bishops). If we read the various resolutions of the

Lambeth Conferences, decennial meetings of Anglican bishops under the direction of the Archbishop of Canterbury, we will note that this requirement of an episcopate is a constant for our Anglican brethren. And the same thing might be said of our Orthodox and Old Catholic brethren. However union between Anglicans and Protestants be blueprinted, this requirement of an episcopate always turns up. Thus an Anglican, an Orthodox, or an Old Catholic cannot conceive of unity otherwise than as guaranteed by and built upon the episcopal ministry, whatever be in other respects the more or less democratic conception of this episcopal ministry which they can arrive at.

Thus when they direct to God the intentions common to all Christians, the faithful of these Churches will keep in their hearts the thought that the unity for which they are praying will be achieved within the framework, however flexible, of their Church. This is not to say that they are praying that all Christians will become Anglicans, or Orthodox, or Old Catholics, in the strict and historical sense of these terms; but it does mean that they will hope that all Christians will grasp the necessity of the episcopal office in the Church, and that, in one way or another, Protestant ministers will be ingrafted into the apostolic succession by some completion of their ordination or by a ceremony of mutual benediction which will render their ministry, at present valid from some points of view, really Catholic, really universal, and valid in every part of Christianity.

We cannot blame our brethren of these Churches for this particular conviction. In it they reveal to us an aspect of the structure of the Church which we are neglecting—perhaps mistakenly. Furthermore, we cannot reproach them for it, given that they believe—and herein lies a connection between them and Protestants—that this episcopal structure was contained already in the organization of the Church described by the New Testament. Faithfulness to the Bible, then, and loyalty to the primitive Church which emerged from the apostolic age, causes them to insist on this need of an episcopal structure providing a framework for, a validity to, all the Church's ministries. But it is also striking, when we read of the various Lambeth Conferences, to see how much this notion of the need of an episcopate can be enriched, developed, nuanced; though it remains intact, it has been brought within the scope of the requirements of unity. The Anglican Church has here made a remarkable effort. And the Anglican faithful can, in their prayer, make room for all these nuances, for all these possible adaptations of the episcopal requirement. But, to repeat, this requirement is insisted upon; there would be no real Catholic loyalty were there no loyalty to this particular conception of Christian ecclesiology.

As for the Orthodox, we meet the same episcopal requirement there; and to it must be added dogmatic and liturgical requirements: acceptance of the first seven ecumenical councils, a common prayer of the Church affording place for the mystery—understood in the sense of the Fathers of the Church—of a highly developed sacramental life, and a theology of the Holy Spirit as alone able to quicken our present-day Church life.

3) *Roman convictions*

A Roman Catholic would simply stop being a Roman Catholic if his prayer for unity obliged him to renounce the dogmas which are the basis of his Catholic belief. We are not thinking here of the dogmas we have in common, constituents today of our visible unity, but of the dogmas defined after the Reformation—for instance, certain Marian and certain ecclesiological ones. Of these, we shall limit ourselves here to emphasizing the doctrine of papal infallibility. We cannot ask a Roman Catholic to envision the form unity will take otherwise than affording a place to the papacy and to an infallible pope. A Roman Catholic, though his prayer for unity is perfectly docile and truly offered via the sovereign intention of Jesus Christ, thinks that unity will finally take place through the acceptance by all Christians of the authority and infallibility of the pope. Assuredly, in his prayer for unity, accompanied by this particular conviction about papal infallibility, the Roman Catholic may hope that this dogma will one day (at the time of a general council, for example) be explained in, or fitted into, the general doctrine on Church and council.

The Roman Catholic may reflect on all the rearrangements that may be made by the Second Vatican Council to bestow more authority on local bishops in the Roman Catholic Church, underlining the fact that the Catholic Church is an ensemble of local, bishop-headed Churches grouped around the similarly local-episcopal Church of Rome, headed by the pope. In this way, the particular Roman Catholic conviction of which we have been speaking may not, after all, require an immediate reconciliation with the organization of the Roman Catholic Church which exists at this moment. A Roman Catholic, then, may reflect that—in view of the present-day development of the Church and in view particularly of the existence of the Second Vatican Council—the particular Roman requirement of which we speak may become something more pliable—something that other separated Christians may find less opaque. But, when all is said and done, the genuine Roman Catholic will think that visible unity will somehow have to be guaranteed and manifested by the authority and infallibility of the pope.

Yet it must be repeated that these *particular* convictions which we cannot exclude from our prayer for unity remain within the compass and the light of our *common* intentions and of our docility, above all, which consists in uniting truly with the intention of Jesus Christ on the eve of his passion when he prayed to the Father. Our sovereign prayer for unity asks the Holy Spirit to place in our hearts and on our lips the same intention and the same intention and the same prayer as Jesus Christ's, who petitioned the Father: "That they may all be one; that they may be one in us, as thou, Father, art in me, and I in thee; so that the world may come to believe that it is thou who has sent me."

Who can pretend to know today exactly what Christ was thinking when he was saying this prayer? As already explained, we cannot get away from our particular convictions, our particular ecclesiological focus. But when we enter truly into the prayer of Jesus Christ, we must surrender totally to him and realize—for to no Christian's belief is this contrary—that God's will, Christ's intention, and the Holy Spirit's prayer in us infinitely surpass anything we could think of to ask for. Thus, totally surrendering ourselves and all that we are and all our ecclesiological conceptions and all our dogmatic certainties to the will of Jesus Christ praying to his Father for unity, we shall be intimately united with that whole cloud of witnesses of every time and of every place who, grouped at this instant around the throne of God, utter the true prayer for unity, the exact words and final intentions of which must remain unknown to us here.

THANKSGIVING AND INTERCESSION FOR UNITY IN THE EUCHARIST

When in our separated Churches we celebrate the Lord's Supper we must more than at any other time be struck by the sadness of our division. That this sacrament of unity should have become a bone of contention and that we may not share the same communion, the same Bread and the same Wine, the sacrament of the Body and Blood of Christ—this is a scandal. Nevertheless, our Eucharist is the work of God in our Churches; and in our celebration of the Sacred Banquet, we are drawn by the Holy Spirit, in Christ, to give thanks to the Father. To this thanksgiving we can unite all our joy at having refound our separated brothers, at understanding them today better than ever before, and at approaching the unity which the Lord has prepared for us together with them. If, then, our Eucharist touches the raw spot of our divisions, it enables us at the same time to thank God for all the marvels he has accomplished in Jesus Christ and through the Holy Spirit, and most especially for this latest marvel—the unity which is growing among us.

Our Eucharist is also the place where we can offer with the greatest fervor and the greatest intensity our intercession for the whole Church and for the whole world. Indeed, by the Holy Supper we are placed in the presence of Christ's sacrifice—we are met at the foot of the cross and there, with the Crucified, we can offer up to God a fervent prayer for his Church and for the world.

Our Lord Jesus Christ stands at this very instant before the face of the Father to intercede in our behalf. United with this intercession, in the Lord's Supper more than in any other office of the Church we can be certain of being heard and of receiving a blessing of Godspeed upon the path to visible and final unity. United to the cross of Christ, united to our heavenly High Priest, we can offer to the Father the sovereign intention of our unity. Despite our divisions we can truly celebrate today the Eucharist for unity, keeping in our intentions, in our mementos, all our separated brethren and in particular those who are members of their various hierarchies, with their weighty responsibilities, and also in particular all workers for unity both in the field of theology and in the field of concrete activity.

In the Eucharist, in all our eucharistic liturgies, there is one moment called the fraction or breaking of the bread when the bread is divided for the communion of all. We can recall at that moment that unhappily this fraction is not the division of the eucharistic bread for all our brethren who are still separated in their communion of the Body and Blood of Christ. This moment of the fraction can, then, be for us the moment of a particular pang of sorrow for our division. But at the same time this moment of the fraction can be a sign of our hope.

For is not the bread that we break the communion of the Body of Christ, and the cup of thanksgiving the communion of the Blood of Christ? We are incorporated into the Body of Christ and believe that in this Eucharist we are really nourished by this Body. We are quickened by the Blood of Christ which has redeemed us, and believe that in the Eucharist this Blood of Christ revivifies the whole Church. "The one bread makes us one body, though we are many in number; the same bread is shared by all." This word of St. Paul's, giving full significance to the eucharistic fraction, is an occasion for us to hunger after unity, for we have not all part together in this one bread. But it is also full of hope, for if in our particular Churches we form one single body, having together a share in the one single bread, we can hope that Christ (who sees his Church as a unity) will conduct us via our Eucharists—still separated—towards the great banquet of unity, the Eucharist broken and shared among all Christians when they have refound their visible unity.

And beyond this visible unity of the Eucharist we proceed towards the great banquet of the Kingdom to come where our Lord will gather us all together in one single community for all eternity. At the moment, then, of the eucharistic fraction we can recall that we are fractions still, but that this fragmentation is in the process of disappearing, thanks to the common intention of prayer for unity carried on in Christ, dictated by the Holy Spirit and ascending to the Father of the one single Christian family. At this eucharistic fraction, at the moment when the bread is broken, we can in spirit bring all our separated brethren around the altar and beg the Lord that one day all these Christian brethren, when they are together in the same place, will be able to receive the same bread, the same sacrament of the Body and Blood of Christ.

Lord Jesus Christ, who didst say to thine apostles, Peace I leave unto you, my peace I give you; look not upon our sins, but upon the faith of thy Church, and as thou didst desire—in accordance with thy will—grant it peace, and gather it together into the unity thou desirest for it; for thou livest and reignest world without end. Amen.